C·L·A·S·S·I·C
RACING CARS

Grand Prix and Indy

C·L·A·S·S·I·C
RACING CARS

Grand Prix and Indy

David Hodges

Chelsea House Publishers
Philadelphia

Acknowledgements

Most of the photographs in this book are from David Hodges' Collection, and the Publisher is also grateful to the Alfa Romeo Centro Storico, *Autocar* Archives, *Autosport,* Neill Bruce and the Peter Roberts Collection, The Ford Motor Company, IGN, Indianapolis Motor Speedway, Mercedes-Benz, Mobil, David Phipps, Proaction (Philip Morris/Marlboro), Maurice Rowe and David Windsor.

Front cover pictures:
McLaren M23 and Penske PC3, driven by James Hunt and John Watson (inset, Penske PC23).

Back cover:
Lotus 78.

Page 2:
The start of the French Grand Prix 1994.

Page 3:
The classic photograph of Ray Harroun's Marmon Wasp at Indianapolis in 1911. This was the first single-seater to win a major race, the first '500'.

Published in 1998 by
Chelsea House Publishers
1974 Sproul Road, Suite 400, P.O. Box 914
Broomall, PA 19008-0914

Library of Congress Cataloging-in-Publication Data applied for

ISBN 0-7910-4999-X

Printed in China

Contents

Introduction

This book traces the development of racing cars over three-quarters of a century, through a series of profiles describing cars, or groups of cars, and recalling their successes.

The first quarter of a century of motor sport was a formative period, when progress was often measured by yardsticks from the heroic age of racing over open roads, and faster and faster speeds were achieved with larger and larger engines. Just before the First World War, there was a noticeable increase in sophistication. Another watershed came just after the war, as a separate sports car category gained in recognition and popularity. Occasionally, there would be interchange, but broadly speaking, the evolution of the cars that were soon to be classified as single-seaters and the sports cars that were raced followed gently diverging paths.

So while some of the early Grand Prix and Indianapolis cars are recalled with illustrations, the cars from the years following the First World War have been chosen for the opening chapters. This is in no way intended to underestimate the efforts of the pioneers, or the men who crewed

LEFT
The first Grand Prix. Ferenc Szisz waiting to start his 13-litre Renault at Le Mans in June 1906. Ahead of him was a two-day race, with 769 miles of hard driving over poor roads. He won at 62.88 mph.

the cars, who raced on roads that were often no better than a modern rally's forest special stage, and at speeds that were then astonishing.

The 1920s was a decade when Grand Prix and U.S. track racing regulations briefly coincided, as they did only occasionally in later years. After the 1920s, the pace of racing car development was usually forced in the Grand Prix world. From the 1960s, this was increasingly centred in Britain, to an extent that would have astonished earlier generations – the time even came when the overwhelming majority of Indianapolis cars and engines were 'Made in England', regardless of the names or badges they carried at the Speedway and Indycar race venues.

Some of the cars described were technical landmarks, some were run-of-the-mill in technical respects but were successful on the circuits, but most are included on both counts. Inevitably, other cars have been left out, but the fifty or more included – if groups are taken into account – are a representative cross-section of three-quarters of a century of sometimes astonishing achievement.

LEFT
The 1914 Grand Prix Mercedes was sound, rather than innovative, but with the backing of exemplary preparation and team work was a convincing winner in that year's Grand Prix. This type later won at Indianapolis and in the Targa Florio at the other end of the racing spectrum.

RIGHT
The Duesenbergs waiting for the start of the 1921 French GP. Unusually among GP cars, these were left-hand drive cars.

BELOW and OPPOSITE
Duesenbergs for road and track. The 3-litre straight eight caused consternation in France when Jimmy Murphy drove it to a clear victory in the 1921 French GP. In 1925 Peter DePaolo won the Indianapolis 500 with this supercharged 2-litre straight eight, averaging 101.13 mph.

Duesenberg Straight Eights

The last Grand Prix before the First World War was won by a car that echoed Edwardian practices, but when the race was revived it was dominated by up-to-the-minute cars. The principal contenders had straight eight engines, and four-wheel brakes were universal. One thing did not change – French vanity took a terrible battering in 1914, and again in 1921.

In France, Ballot's straight eight was designed by Ernest Henry, and despite hasty preparation, it showed well in the 1919 Indianapolis 500. Then that race was subject to 183 cu in regulations that were adopted as the 3-litre GP formula in 1921. A Ballot was second in the '500' in 1920, and de Palma drove one to win the Elgin National, before the marque faded from US racing.

Brothers Fred and August Duesenberg built a racing eight that was simpler than Ballot's, in that it was a single-cam unit. Reflecting track

intentions, the Duesenbergs also had three-speed gearboxes. The first cars were completed late for the 1920 Indianapolis 500, but placed 3-4-6, and they were 2-4-6 in 1921. Two of the cars run there were then included in Duesenberg's four-car entry for the French GP, where Duesenberg had one great advantage – the first four-wheel hydraulic brakes in GP racing. Ballot led only six of the 30 GP laps. Jimmy Murphy nursed his battered Duesey through the closing laps to win at 78.1 mph, with team mates fourth and sixth at the end of a gruelling race.

After that, Duesenberg stayed at home, duelling with Miller for most of the 1920s. The last 183 cu in '500', in 1922, fell to a Miller-engined Duesenberg (and there were seven true Duesenbergs in the top ten). The first Duesenberg win came in 1924, and also in the same year the winning Duesey was the first to win the '500' at over 100 mph.

WINNER. Average 101 13 per hour.
PETE DePAOLO IN DUESENBERG
13th Annual 500 Mile Race
Indianapolis Motor Speedway
MAY 30th 1925.

WON ON FIRESTONE GUM DIPPED BALLOON CORDS AND STEAM WELDED TUBES.

Alfa Romeo P2

The Alfa Romeo P2 appeared solid behind its 'bull-nose' radiator, but the car was aerodynamically efficient by the standards of the mid-1920s.

This first car to carry the Alfa Romeo name into Grand Prix racing laid a firm foundation for marque legends, that are still alive seven decades later. A car with the preceding ALFA name had failed to start in the 1914 GP, then the P1 of 1923 was abandoned after a fatal test accident. Nicola Romeo then used Enzo Ferrari as his intermediary to lure talented Fiat engineer, Vittorio Jano, to his company to design the P2.

This followed Fiat practices in its chassis and non-independent suspension, and in its straight eight, a twin-cam 1987 cc unit with a Roots-type supercharger, initially rated at 134 bhp, and in its second year at 155 bhp. Fiat resemblances were not so close as the famous 1923 Sunbeam 'Fiat-in-green-paint' GP car. Fiat copies that beat Fiats led Giovanni Agnelli to withdraw Fiat from racing, save for an advanced but short-lived 1927 project.

Antonio Ascari drove a P2 to a debut race victory, and tyre failure cost Giuseppe Campari another race before the all-important French GP at Lyon in August 1924. Campari won that 503-mile classic at 71 mph, then Ascari headed an Alfa 1-2-3 in the Italian GP.

The next year brought triumph in the European GP, but tragedy as Ascari was killed in the French GP. The modified P2s won the Italian GP, that victory gaining the first World Championship for Alfa Romeo. Since then, the Alfa badge has been circled by a laurel wreath ...

After 1925 the P2s were not eligible for GP racing, but modified and with engines giving up to 175 bhp were still successful and they were eventually run by Scuderia Ferrari. In 1930 Varzi scored the last great P2 victory, in the Targa Florio.

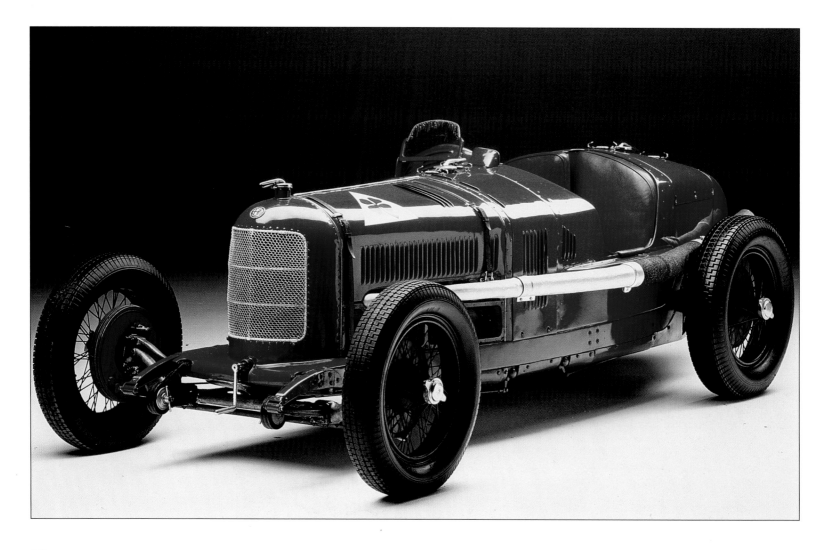

Bugatti Type 35

The real basis for legends is often shaky, and overall Ettore Bugatti was not a very successful Grand Prix constructor. However, his supremely elegant Type 35 and its derivatives were vitally important to GP racing through the late 1920s, when there were no other teams of 'works' stature, and the only other GP cars available to independent entrants were handed-down models from mid-decade. Following Harry Miller, Bugatti pioneered the manufacture of top-class racing cars for sale, and his T35s, T35Bs, T35Cs and T39s became widely used at every level of racing.

The 24-valve sohc straight eight followed the engine used in the unsuccessful 1922-23 GP Bugattis, with a modest power output of 95 bhp in its first 1991 cc form. Bugatti considered supercharging 'unethical', but for 1926 fitted a supercharger to the 1492 cc T39 engine, and that unit gave 110 bhp. The channel-section main chassis members varied in depth, to meet anticipated stresses. Bugatti used his normal non-independent suspension, in combination with the rigid chassis and these cars had good road-holding and handling.

With its carefully proportioned body, the T35 stands out among classic racing cars today, as it did when it made its debut in the 1924 French GP. There it was outclassed by formidable

opponents, but between 1926 and 1931 the T35/T39 won 68 major races, including 14 national Grands Prix. Coupled with the artistry of its design, that record more than justifies its status.

ABOVE, BELOW, NEXT PAGE
The Bugatti T35 was a handsome little car, slender so that its cockpit was cramped, and notable for its unique cast-alloy wheels with integral brake drums. The whole car, especially the engine compartment, displayed the craftsmanship for which the company was renowned. Bugatti engines were never outstandingly powerful, but always had symmetry and visual appeal.

Miller Straight Eights

Harry Armenius Miller built racing cars for sale, seemingly with little concern for commercial aspects, but with every regard for quality. In the 1920s, Miller straight eights were America's finest track cars, and among the most sophisticated racing machines anywhere in the world. As the decade opened, Miller was commissioned to build an engine to challenge Duesenberg's eight. These Miller cars had some successes in 1921-22, and Jimmy Murphy won the 1922 Indianapolis 500 with a Miller-engined Duesenberg.

Miller provided the inspiration, Leo Goosens the working designs, and production engineer Fred Offenhauser built the cars. For the 122 cu in (2-litre) American regulations these were ultra-slim single-seaters, for the AAA dropped its requirement for a riding mechanic in 1923-29. The elegant twin overhead camshaft engine was beefed-up, and Miller in 1925 added a centrifugal supercharger. The 122 Millers were strong contenders on U.S. tracks (including board speedways) and in record attempts. Count Louis Zborowski's car, one of the few with a two-seater body, was the first independent entry to be admitted to the French Grand Prix (competing without distinction in 1924).

For the 91 cu in (1.5-litre) regulations, Miller built 'conventional' cars and a front-wheel drive version, both with the supercharged eight in 1478 cc form, giving some 154 bhp in 1926 and 252 bhp in normal state of tune only a year later. Although never effective on road circuits, 'pull' rather than 'push' gave some advantages on tracks, where the centrifugal supercharger (effective only at constant high engine speeds) and three-speed gearbox were not drawbacks. Conventional 91s were more successful, with three Indianapolis 500 victories, but in 1927-28 a dozen major U.S. races fell to the more costly fwd cars. Miller's eight-cylinder engines were used on into the 1930s in other cars.

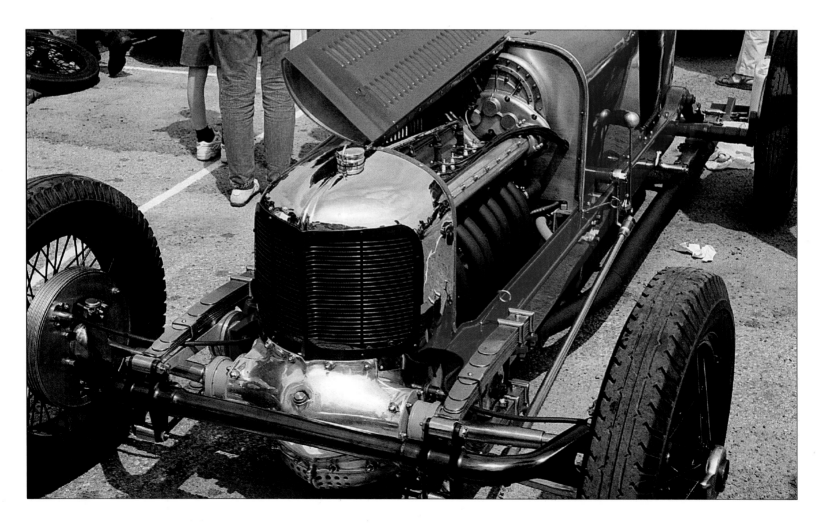

Frank S Lockhart

Winner 1st Place.
Frank Lockhart Miller Special

Pete DePaolo - Boyle Valve Special
Indianapolis Motor Speedway
1929

ABOVE and LEFT
Conventional Millers were
successful track cars in the 1920s,
and Frank Lockhart drove this one
to victory at Indianapolis in 1926.
Peter DePaolo's 1929 Miller entry
for the 500 shows how much lower
the front-wheel drive car was.
Both cars are on 'balloon' tyres.

Delage V12

Louis Delage was a flamboyant self-made man who enjoyed racing, but he allowed it to become one of the activities that over-extended his resources. His cars were successful in racing before the First World War, the 6.2-litre GP machines of 1913 challenged for victory in the French Grand Prix, with one winning at Indianapolis in 1914. In contrast, the 1914 GP Delage was technically advanced, but a racing failure.

Delage returned to Grand Prix racing in 1923 with a V12, when the effective racing straight eight was still fresh. Designer Planchon sought to exploit advantages such as high piston area, in an engine that revved to 7000 rpm, and the first V12 he designed was on a start grid in less than five months. It was a complex 60 degree unit, with twin camshafts gear-driven from the front. In 1923 in normally-aspirated form, it gave some 120 bhp; apparently Louis Delage was not impressed, Planchon was replaced, and Albert Lory took over the engine's development. Lory added twin superchargers, to lift output above 190 bhp for 1925, substantially more than rival eights.

The one car to start in the 1923 French GP, failed to reach quarter distance, but in the 1924 French race there was a team finish, second, third and sixth, and the Delages were then third and fourth in the Spanish GP.

None of the V12s in the 1925 Belgian GP finished. Then there was a 1-2 in the French race, Benoist and Divo sharing the winning drive. That was followed in the Spanish GP by a runaway 1-2-3 in the V12 Delage's last race.

Alfa Romeo Tipo B

The supreme Grand Prix car of the classic period, Vittorio Jano's Alfa Romeo Tipo B 'Monoposto' – usually known as the P3 – was designed for the 1932 formula, which limited race duration to five hours, but imposed no restrictions on engine size. It was an economy design, but it won first time out and carried the hopes of Italy into the first years of the '750 kg formula' which saw the emergence of powerful German teams.

In 1932 the GP regulations no longer called for space for a second seat (racing mechanics had been banned in 1925!) so the P3 was the first GP car with a single-seat cockpit on the centre line – hence the name 'Monoposto'.

The 8C 'Monza' had been used in GPs as well as sports car races, but was under-powered.

As a completely new design was out of the question, Jano drew on the Monza in the P3. The straight eight had two cylinder blocks on a common crankcase, with a one-piece dohc cylinder head. A train of gears between the blocks drove the camshafts, pumps and the two superchargers, one on each side, each feeding a group of cylinders. Supercharger boost was modest (roughly 10.5 lb sq in) and in its first 2654 cc form the engine was rated at 215 bhp; in the face of the German onslaught it was to be enlarged to 2.9 litres, then 3.2 litres (and 265 bhp) and eventually to 3.8 litres. In that form, the claimed output of 330 bhp was 100 bhp less than the 1935 Mercedes.

Jano used a conventional chassis of pressed-steel side members and rigid axles with the

BELOW
Classic line up – the Scuderia Ferrari 'P3' team before the 1934 French GP at Montlhéry, when they triumphed over the German newcomers, in a false dawn. Drivers are Achille Varzi, race winner Louis Chiron and Count Felice Trossi.

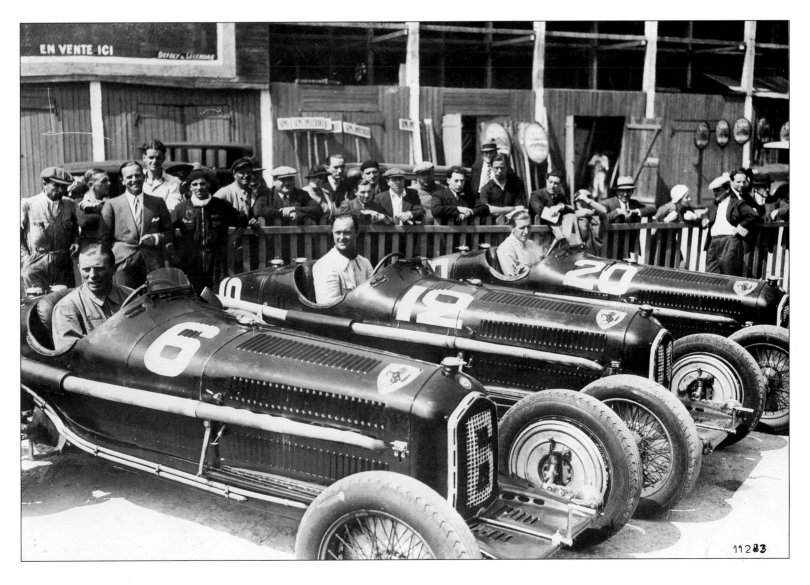

unique feature of a twin propeller shaft transmission. From a differential immediately behind the engine/gearbox, two angled shafts took the power to bevel final drives inboard of the wheels. This reduced unsprung weight, as the axle linking the two could be light, and improved traction.

Tazio Nuvolari won the 1932 Italian and French GPs, and three secondary Italian races, while Caracciola won the German and Monza GPs. Then Alfa Romeo was forced to withdraw from racing, leaving Scuderia Ferrari to uphold the marque's honour with uprated Monzas. These were not reliable, and in the high summer of 1933 Ferrari eventually persuaded Alfa Romeo to release the P3s to his team. It scored six out of six in the remaining races, Louis Chiron and Luigi Fagioli winning three apiece.

In 1934 the cars had to be modified to meet the new regulations, and at first all went well. Guy Moll won at Monaco and drove a streamlined car to win on Berlin's AVUS track, while in the first full Grand Prix confrontation Chiron headed an Alfa 1-2-3, as the German teams collapsed in the French GP. There was also a Targa Florio victory, but in the main Grand Prix arena the German teams then found reliability.

For 1935 Ferrari enlarged the engines, introduced independent front suspension and revised the rear suspension. There were wins in secondary races, and in July Nuvolari drove an inspired race to beat the Germans in their home GP at the Nürburgring. That was one high point in his career, and perhaps the high point in the Alfa Romeo Tipo B story.

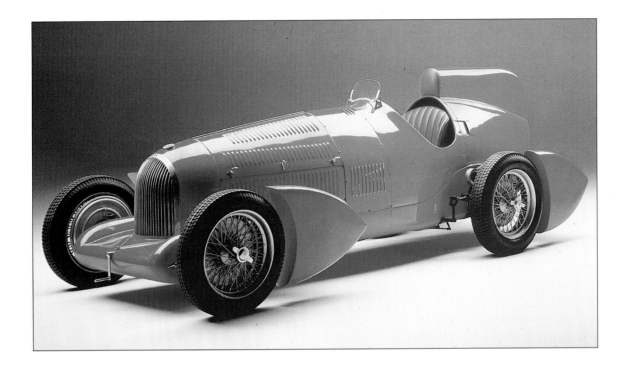

LEFT
This very special Tipo B
Aerodinamica was prepared for
track racing in 1934.

19

Mercedez-Benz W25 – W154

A new Grand Prix formula for 1934, and the announcement of German State rewards for GP success, led to the 1933 Mercedes-Benz decision to make a comeback in top-flight racing. Through the rest of the 1930s its cars were to set new standards, matched only by a new German rival, Auto Union, while the French effort was wiped out and the Italians usually relegated to supporting roles.

Mercedes' W25 for 1934 was built to rules stipulating a maximum car weight of 750 kg (1652 lb), without liquids and tyres, and with the W25s this was just achieved, once by scraping the paint off. The car brought together independent suspension all round, hydraulic brakes and a gearbox integral with the final drive – nothing new, but new in combination. The twin-cam straight eight supercharged engine followed orthodox Mercedes lines. In 3.36 litre form it gave over 320 bhp (but was slightly detuned for races), and it was enlarged in three steps to 4.3 litres in the 1935 M25C form, when it produced some 400 bhp in race trim.

In 1934 these Mercedes won two GPs and two secondary races, and the team experienced galling defeats. However, in 1935 it was beaten only four times, Rudolf Caracciola winning six races and Luigi Fagioli three.

The 1936 short-chassis car with a 4.74-litre, 470-plus bhp engine, was a failure – after two early-season victories, it was consistently beaten, and performances were so poor that Mercedes-Benz withdrew its entries for the last three races.

A new racing department under Rudolf Uhlenhaut laid down the W125 for the last year of the 750 kg formula. This had a stiffer oval-tube frame and a de Dion rear axle (in place of the W25 swing axles). The 5.66-litre straight eight had a new supercharger arrangement and a racing output of around 570 bhp, enough to put Mercedes back on top in 1937, when the team won seven races to Auto Union's five (Carraciola won four, rising new driver Hermann Lang two, Manfred von Brauchitsch one).

For the 3-litre Grands Prix of 1938-39, Mercedes discarded the eight-in-line

arrangement, developing a 60 degree four-cam V12, which gave 425 bhp early in 1938 and over 480 bhp with two-stage supercharging in 1939. It was installed in a chassis derived from the 1937 car, with softer suspension.

This combination of power and efficiency brought Mercedes six victories in 1938 – including the only 1930s GP win for a British driver, Richard Seaman, in the German GP – but Nuvolari won the last two races for Auto Union. The 1939 results were similar, Lang winning five times for Mercedes, and Carraciola once, while Auto Union took two races.

In 1947 one car was entered privately for the Indianapolis 500. This car ran as high as fourth before retiring, and it ran again in 1948, when its complexities defeated its American crew. Then in 1951, Mercedes sent a team to run in two Argentine races, where they were humbled by Gonzalez in an independent 2-litre Ferrari. Time had caught up with the mightiest of the 'Silver Arrows'.

LEFT
Prestige meant that both German teams of the 1930s prepared very special streamlined cars for races at Berlin's AVUS track. This W125 on the brick-surfaced banking is being tested before the 1937 race.

BELOW
For many years the W125 was rated the most powerful GP car, although that was based on a test output of 646 bhp that was never achieved in a race-tune engine. It certainly looked the part, and gave Mercedes the upper hand in 1937.

LEFT
The 12-cylinder engine of the Mercedes W154, with the covers of its four cams prominent above each bank, was slightly angled in the chassis so that the propeller shaft passed alongside the driver's seat.

RIGHT
A D-type Auto Union at a Silverstone historic meeting in the 1990s, with a Mercedes-Benz W154 adversary from 1939 behind it. Compared to earlier Auto Unions this was a sophisticated car, but slender resources and driver changes meant that it was never fully developed, or exploited.

Auto Union

The mid-engined racing car layout is taken for granted now, but it has been accepted in every major category for no more than a quarter of a century. The breakthrough might have come in the 1930s, if Mercedes-Benz had not been more successful with Grand Prix cars on more conventional lines, generally gaining the upper hand over Auto Union's cars with their engines behind the drivers.

Auto Union was a consortium of four minor manufacturers which came together in 1932; DKW, Horch and Wanderer disappeared, Audi survived, and perpetuated the four linked rings badge of the original quartet. By 1933 Auto Union was turning to GP racing to publicize its existence. Wanderer employed a free-thinking consultant, Dr Ferdinand Porsche; his associate Adolf Rosenberger had raced the short-lived rear-engined Benz cars in 1923, and other key men in the GP programme were engine designer Josef Kales, and chassis expert Karl Rabe.

The Auto Union 'P-Wagen' or A type, was a spectacularly unconventional machine. Its supercharged 4.36-litre 45 degree V16 had a single camshaft, between the cylinder bank heads. It was lazy and lightly stressed, rated at no more than 295 bhp at 4500 rpm. It was behind the cockpit in a chassis of two large tubes and cross members. There was torsion-bar independent front suspension and swing axles at the rear, the gearbox was behind the back wheels and the fuel tank was between cockpit and engine at the centre of gravity, so that handling would remain consistent as its load was used.

Drivers had to learn new techniques, as the team found its feet. But in the second half of 1934 there were three GP victories, scored by Hans Stuck. As the B-type, the design was reworked with torsion bar rear suspension and a 4.95-litre engine for 1935, when there was a GP victory in Italy, and brilliant newcomer Berndt Rosemeyer won the Czech GP.

The 1936 C-type was essentially similar, but with 6-litre 520 bhp engines. Rosemeyer won five races, Varzi one. Then fortunes swung to Mercedes again. For Auto Union Hasse and von Delius each won a race, but success increasingly depended on Rosemeyer, whose four 1937

victories included the Vanderbilt Cup in the U.S.A. and the last race of the 750 kg formula, the Donington Grand Prix.

For the 3-litre formula, Robert Eberan von Eberhorst designed a new car with advances such as de Dion rear suspension and 60 degree V12, giving 420 bhp at 7000 rpm in 1938, 485 bhp with two-stage supercharging in 1939. It had one central camshaft operating all the inlet valves, and individual camshafts on each bank for the exhaust valves.

The loss of Rosemeyer in a futile record attempt before the 1938 racing season was a great blow. Auto Union missed the early races, then Tazio Nuvolari was persuaded to join the team, and late in the year he won the Italian and Donington GPs. Stuck won a race in 1939, Nuvolari beat the Mercedes in the Yugoslavia GP, run on the day the Second World War started. Auto Unions never raced again, and the next GP victory for a mid-engined car did not come until 1958, when Stirling Moss drove a Cooper to win in Argentina.

Berndt Rosemeyer in full flight at the Nürburgring in a 6-litre C-type Auto Union. He had been a racing motorcyclist and came to these rear-engined cars with no preconceived ideas of racing car handling, so he adapted to them more easily than some established drivers.

RIGHT
The D-type had its cockpit further back in the wheelbase than earlier Auto Unions. The triple-camshaft engine layout and two-stage supercharger show well, as do the pleasing curves of the bodywork.

The Auto Union as it first appeared in 'A' form in 1934, when its unorthodoxy baffled the racing world. Some of the air scoops on this car appear to have been additions after trials, and the nationalistic emblem was seldom carried outside Germany after hostile receptions. An external starter engaged the shaft projecting at the rear.

Maserati 8C

The Maserati brothers' shoestring racing car boutique at Bologna concentrated on second-level cars once the strength of the mid-1930s German onslaught on the Grands Prix was appreciated. Then a take-over by industrialist Adolfo Orsi meant there was a budget to develop a 3-litre car for the 1938 formula. This 8C became better-known at Indianapolis, with two '500' victories to its credit.

The budget did not run to a complex car. The 2992 cc 8CTF engine was made up of two four-cylinder blocks (from the 1.5-litre cars) with a one-piece cylinder head and Roots-type supercharger. It gave 350 bhp in 1938, while the 32-valve straight eight in the 8CL was a little more potent. There was a welded box-section chassis and one novelty was the cast aluminium oil tank, which served as chassis cross-bracing and supported the fuel tank and seat.

In 1938 the 8C proved fast – Trossi led the mighty Mercedes team in two events – but fragile. Its best GP placing came in 1939, when Pietsch led the German GP, and finished third.

By that time the 8C was a winner, in a different world. In 1938 Mike Boyle ordered an 8C for Wilbur Shaw to race at Indianapolis; as the 'Boyle Special' this 8C was carefully prepared and supercharger boost reduced, to improve reliability.

Shaw drove it to win the 1939 500, the first win for a European car since 1919, it won again in 1940 and seemed to be heading for a third victory in 1941 when a wheel failed.

All four 8CTFs and the 8CL ran in the 1940 500, then in 1946 and 1947 Ted Horn placed the Boyle car third, and he was fourth in 1948. Villoresi was seventh in a new 8CL in 1946 and later drove this car to win a secondary Argentine road race. 8Cs lingered at Indianapolis until 1951, albeit showing their age.

The 8CTF Maserati seemed simple alongside its 1938 German rivals, but it was advanced by Indianapolis standards and gained a splendid record in track racing.

Alfa Romeo 158/159

German domination of Grand Prix racing in the late 1930s led Enzo Ferrari to recommend that Alfa Romeo enter the second-level voiturette category – at the time, his Scuderia Ferrari ran the front-line Alfas, although that arrangement was to end in 1938, soon after the Tipo 158 had been laid down. Ferrari was to set up as an independent constructor, and 13 years after the Alfa 158 he had initiated had made its debut, his GP cars ended its career.

Alfa designer Gioacchino Colombo was seconded to the 158 project, to work at Ferrari's Modena base. This straightforward car was built around a supercharged straight eight (158 – 1.5-litres, eight cylinders). It was a 1479 cc twin overhead camshaft unit, with a Roots-type supercharger and produced 180 bhp in its first tests. In 1939 it was rated at 225 bhp, and with two-stage supercharging the eventual output was up to 425 bhp, with a prodigious thirst for fuel that was 98 per cent methanol.

There was a simple twin-tube chassis and the suspension was independent, with transverse leaf springs all round, and swing axles at the rear.

As the 'Alfetta', the 158s won first time out (at Leghorn in August 1938), they had teething problems, but won again, then suffered an embarrassing defeat by Mercedes in the 1939 Tripoli GP. Six 158Cs were built for 1940 – when there was a team 1-2-3 at Tripoli and Mercedes' records were broken – these cars survived the Second World War, hidden with most of the racing equipment, in a village in the foothills of the Alps. Thus the Alfa Corse team had competitive cars ready when proper racing resumed in 1946, and the 158s automatically became Grand Prix cars in 1947 as new regulations were introduced (for 1½-litre supercharged or 4½-litre normally aspirated engines).

Component failures led to retirements in the 158's first 1946 race, but then came a run of victories that lasted until 1951. In 1947 Italian veterans Varzi and Trossi and French driver Jean-

158s rampant in the first race of the modern World Drivers' Championship, at Silverstone in 1950. Giuseppe Farina, leading team mate Fagioli in this shot, won the race and the first title.

LEFT
As more and more power was squeezed from the straight eight, the Alfa's fuel consumption became excessive, to the point where a 159 driver was surrounded by fuel tanks. These show in this stripped car in the Alfa Romeo museum.

BELOW
The leading car of the post-Second World War racing revival, the Alfa Romeo 158 became as familiar as its 'P3' predecessor had been in the 1930s. It was not a complex car, and that was reflected in its no-nonsense lines.

Pierre Wimille won four races; Wimille won three times in 1948, when Alfa's fourth victory fell to Trossi. Then the team took a year out.

They were back in 1950, for a golden season in that first year of the modern World Championship. For Alfa Romeo, Giuseppe Farina won the British, Swiss and Italian GPs, and became champion; team-mate Juan-Manuel Fangio won the other three title races, in Monaco, Belgium and France, and was runner-up in the championship.

The car was uprated as the 159 to meet a growing Ferrari threat, although by 1951 time was catching up with an old design. Supercharger pressure was increased again, but no less than 135 bhp was absorbed in supercharger drive, and drivers were constrained to use no more than 9000 rpm in races, to ensure reliability. Normal fuel tank capacity was 66 gallons, and still two refuelling stops were called for in a 300-mile championship Grand Prix – consumption was 1.6 mpg! Brakes were improved, a de Dion rear axle was used on some cars, the frame was stiffened ... little more could be done.

Farina and Fangio did win four championship GPs in 1951, and Fangio took the world title, but after 26 consecutive victories, the team at last met defeat at the hands of Ferrari, at Silverstone. At the end of the season Alfa Romeo retired these cars, going out on a high note as Fangio won the Spanish Grand Prix.

Maserati 250F

This was an outstanding car, although its specification suggests no more than a workmanlike machine, and it was one of the last of a long 'traditional' line. Its active career spanned the whole of the seven-year 2½-litre GP formula, and while the 250F score of eight championship race victories seems modest, there were only 28 such events when it was a front-line car, from 1954 until 1957, when the Maserati racing department closed.

Maserati resources were slender, and the 2493 cc dohc straight six engine was developed on the back of the preceding 2-litre unit. It gave some 240 bhp in 1954, and 270 bhp in 1957. There was a multi-tube chassis, with conventional coil spring and wishbone front suspension, and a de Dion arrangement at the rear.

Fangio drove 250Fs to win the car's first GP,

and the next, but a little later in 1954 formidable opposition emerged from Germany, in the shape of the Mercedes W196. During the rest of the season the Maserati won only secondary races. There it perhaps found its true role, for it was an ideal private entrant car, and outstanding among such drivers was Stirling Moss. His driving earned him 'official' status with Maserati, and clinched his Mercedes contract for 1955.

Moss was back with Maserati in 1956, leading the team and winning two GPs despite the car's lack of outright speed, compared with Ferraris. In 1957 Fangio drove Maseratis, and in his last full season won four GPs and the championship.

Lightweight versions, and another with a V12, were never fully developed. Survivors of the 29 cars built were to become mainstays of historic racing.

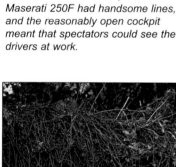

From the Trident motif within the nose to the rounded tail, the Maserati 250F had handsome lines, and the reasonably open cockpit meant that spectators could see the drivers at work.

Mercedez-Benz W196

The great German manufacturer returned to GP racing in 1954 with a car bristling with novelty, and by contemporary standards with generous technical and financial backing – and in the knowledge that failure could hardly be contemplated against Mercedes' background of racing domination.

Typically, a design group was set up following detail feasibility studies. The W196 that made its debut in the French GP was dazzling, with a space frame and the engine laid over at 37 degrees to reduce frontal area, normal i.f.s. and swing axle i.r.s., massive finned drum brakes inboard all round, and a 2496 cc straight eight with direct fuel injection and desmodromic (positively operated) valve gear. The car first raced with full-width bodywork, and won with it on the fast open Reims circuit before it proved an embarrassment at Silverstone; after that, open-

LEFT and ABOVE
The W196 has solid and chunky lines enclosing complicated mechanical elements – some might say 'over-complicated'. Engine air was taken in through the mesh-fronted intake. Mercedes built more than a dozen of these cars to win 9 of the 12 championship races they contested.

wheel bodies were used on all but the fastest circuits.

In 1954, the team relied on the talents of Juan-Manuel Fangio, who won the French, German, Swiss and Italian GPs for it, and drove the highest-placed W196 in the British and Spanish races, while his team mates managed one second place, two thirds and two fourth placings between them.

The cars were refined in detail for 1955, when thoroughness showed in the availability of chassis with three wheelbase lengths. Fangio had a worthier team mate, Stirling Moss. The Argentine champion again won four GPs while Moss headed a team 1-2-3-4 in the British GP and finishing the season as runner-up to Fangio in the Drivers' Championship.

Daimler-Benz retired the Mercedes team at the end of the season, when it had a GP start/win success rate of 75 percent (it is often forgotten that Ferrari had done better in the preceding seasons). The development potential of these 'Silver Arrows' was not fully exploited, but their reputation was in later demonstrations.

Vanwall

As the 1940s ended, British Grand Prix hopes were pinned on the BRM project, but that was becoming so inept that one of its principal supporters, G.A. (Tony) Vandervell, withdrew and set up his own team, using Ferrari 'Thin Wall Specials' as it moved towards building Vanwall cars.

The first of these emerged slowly, with chassis on Cooper lines and a four-cylinder engine designed by Norton engineer Leo Kuzmicki, and reflecting motorcycle practice. A 2490 cc version with fuel injection came in 1955, and was eventually to produce 285 bhp. It powered the familiar GP Vanwall that appeared in 1956, with a space frame designed by Colin Chapman and a striking low-drag body by Frank Costin. For 1957, Chapman laid out a new rear suspension.

By that time the car had shown real promise, when Stirling Moss drove one to win the 1956 Silverstone International Trophy. He led the 1957 Vanwall team, joined by Tony Brooks and Stuart Lewis-Evans. The British GP fell to the Vanwall shared by Brooks and Moss (the former was unwell, and Moss took over when his own car faltered). That was the first all-British victory in a World Championship race, the first in a national Grand Prix since 1923.

Moss won two more championship GPs that year, both in Italy (Vandervell's great desire had been to beat "those bloody red cars"). Despite problems caused by the obligatory switch to Avgas fuel in 1958, Vanwall roundly defeated Ferrari, to win the first Constructors' Championship; Moss and Brooks won three GPs apiece, but were second and third in the Drivers' Championship. Ill health forced Vandervell to end his full campaign, and the remaining Vanwall efforts were half-hearted, with a one-off lightweight GP car.

The high-built Vanwall had a notably efficient body, which was virtually unchanged through three seasons in the front line. This is VW10, the last of this type built.

Ferrari Dino 246

In the final years of the 1950s, Ferrari was on the defensive. It had to give best to Vanwall, and a greater new threat emerged in the form of rear-engined Coopers, as the Italian constructor fielded the last successful main-line GP car with its engine ahead of the cockpit. The cars were named 'Dino' for Ferrari's son, after their V6 ('24' indicating capacity, '6' the number of cylinders).

The basis of the GP engine was a 1½-litre V6 laid out by the great Vittorio Jano, and designed to run on the 130 octane Avgas that became obligatory for GPs from 1958. It was enlarged in stages to 2417 cc in 1957 (rated at 270 bhp). For 1958 GP use, the space frame of the F2 car was uprated, and the rear suspension was to be changed from de Dion to coil spring and wishbone. Ferrari stubbornly stayed with drum brakes, until Mike Hawthorn insisted that discs were fitted to his car late in 1958, and finally a message got through.

These Ferraris were at their best on high-speed circuits, where in the old Ferrari manner, power was all-important. In 1958 Hawthorn won the French GP and piled up enough points with a string of second placings to snatch the Drivers' Championship from Moss; Peter Collins won the British GP.

Tony Brooks won two fast GPs in 1959, the French race at 127.45 mph and the German event on the AVUS track at 143.61 mph, in cars that were uprated to a degree, and had 280 bhp engines. By 1960 the Dino 246 was completely outmoded, but there was one final GP victory when Californian Phil Hill scored his first championship win, in the Italian GP.

Cooper-Climax

The first purpose-built GP Coopers were front-engined cars for the 2-litre races of 1952-53, simple and underpowered, but useful for up-and-coming drivers. For the Formula 2 that came in 1957 Coopers reverted to the mid-engined layout of the 500 cc cars that were the bedrock of the marque's reputation; these F2 cars won 33 of the 51 significant races run through to 1960, almost invariably with Coventry Climax FPF engines. The design philosophy, and the association with Coventry Climax, was meanwhile carried into the Grand Prix world with such success that racing was fundamentally changed, and in time the Cooper influence extended to U.S. track racing.

Leading entrant, Rob Walker set the ball rolling with an engine enlarged to 1960 cc. Jack Brabham placed a T43 sixth in the 1957 Monaco GP, then Stirling Moss won the Argentine GP at the start of the 1958 season, driving Walker's 1.96-litre car. Maurice Trinignant won the Monaco GP with a fractionally larger engine in it, then a 2.2-litre version came, and then a revised block allowed the capacity to be increased to 2495 cc – full Formula 1 size – for 1959.

This was installed in the essentially simple Cooper T51, and drove through a four-speed gearbox (independent cars such as Walker's had five speed boxes). It had a chassis of four sturdy longitudinal tubes, with transverse leaf spring front suspension and coil springs and wishbones i.r.s., and a functional body. Lower weight combined with agility to offset Ferrari's 30-40 bhp power advantage.

Jack Brabham drove Coopers to win the Monaco and British GPs, and the 1959 Drivers' Championship. Moss won the Portuguese and Italian GPs in a Walker car; Bruce McLaren, the works team number two, became the youngest driver (at the age of 22) to win a World Championship event. He won the U.S. GP at Sebring, and then the early-1960 Argentine GP.

Cooper produced the lower T53 for 1960, with a new tubular frame, coil spring suspension all round, and a five-speed gearbox. With a run of five consecutive GP victories Brabham secured his second driver's title, while McLaren was runner-up, and Cooper took its second Constructors' Championship.

The regulations changed, and in 1961 the 1½-litre engines available to Cooper were inadequate. When it achieved parity, with the Coventry Climax FWMV V8, other constructors had seized the initiative with more sophisticated chassis. During the five years of the Formula, only one championship race fell to Cooper, to

BELOW
The 1960 Cooper T53 was a match for any car, even the more powerful Ferraris, on the fastest circuits as well as sinuous tracks where its agility paid dividends. This is Brabham at Reims, where he won the French GP at 131.9 mph.

Bruce McLaren driving a T60 at Monaco in 1962.

After the U.S. Grand Prix late in 1960, a T53 was taken to Indianapolis for exploratory tests. In this 2.5-litre car, Brabham turned in the fastest lap at 144.8 mph, in a year when pole for the 500 had fallen to a 4.2-litre roadster at 146 mph. That led Jim Kimberly to sponsor a Cooper Indianapolis car for 1961. Coventry Climax increased the capacity of the engine to 2750 cc for this T54, which had a slightly longer wheelbase than T53, and suspension and main fuel load offset for the left-only turns at the Speedway. Brabham qualified for row 5, and despite pit-stop problems finished ninth in the '500'. Thus Cooper started the swing towards mid-engined cars in track racing, as it had in the Grands Prix.

RIGHT
Stirling Moss on his way to an historic victory in the 1958 Argentine GP, the first in modern championship racing for a rear-engined car. Walker's T43 Cooper has extra air intakes and a deflector to direct more air to the radiators. Gamesmanship by the Walker pit crew convinced the Ferrari team that Moss would stop to change tyres. He did not, although the tread was worn off the front tyres.

BELOW
The T51 was a dumpy car compared with its T53 successor. A dual purpose Formula 1/Formula 2 car, it brought six GP victories to Cooper. This T51 is running at Silverstone in the 1990s.

Lotus 18

Lotus entered Grand Prix racing with front-engined cars in 1958, with little success, and Colin Chapman had to accept the rear-engined layout. The Lotus 18 was his first car on these lines.

It was a chunky and simple space-frame car, which in Grand Prix form normally had Coventry Climax FPF four-cylinder engines (2.5-litre units in 1960, 1.5-litre versions when the regulations imposed that capacity limit in 1961). It was also used in Formula 2 in 1960, and 125 were built for Formula Junior, where modified Ford 105E engines were usually fitted. The suspension was independent, with coil springs and wishbones, and although some of the members appeared flimsy, the arrangement made for responsive handling and 'put the power on the road' very efficiently.

Innes Ireland drove Team Lotus 18s to win the marque's first F2 and F1 wins (the latter in secondary events), then Stirling Moss drove Walker's independent 18 to Lotus' first GP victory, at Monaco in 1960. He also won the U.S. GP at Riverside, then in 1961 he was the only driver to beat the powerful Ferraris in the world series, with brilliant drives in the Monaco and German GPs. Two future world champions, Jim Clark and John Surtees, made their GP debuts in 18s. The 21 was an uprated 18 (Ireland won Team Lotus' first GP with one in the U.S.A., then new cars designed for V8s made it obsolete). Walker revised the bodies on his 18s; in one of these, fitted with a Coventry Climax V8, Moss' single-seater racing career ended in a near-fatal accident at Goodwood.

The Lotus 18 appeared simple and boxy, and its suspension looked flimsy (save for the fixed-length driveshafts that were part of the rear set-up). But it was an effective car in several categories, in this case as a Grand Prix car. The driver is Innes Ireland, cornering inside a BRM driven by Jo Bonnier.

Lotus 25

ABOVE
The Lotus 25 appeared spindly, but its monocoque chassis was strong and rigid, and the little car set new standards. It was raced from 1962 until 1965, and will forever be associated with Jim Clark, here throwing one round Silverstone in 1964.

In his Lotus 25, Colin Chapman introduced a new concept to Grand Prix racing, one that spread to every other main category, and in principle holds good today. In the second season of 1½-litre GP racing, two British V8s produced power to more than match Ferrari and the short-lived Porsche GP venture, and Lotus' new car with the Coventry Climax 1498 cc FMWV also had road-holding superior to its rivals, with the possible exception of the BRM P57. But this Lotus 24 turned out to be a customer car, as far as Team Lotus was concerned an interim model, for the 1962 Dutch GP saw the debut of the 25, with a chassis that made existing types obsolete overnight.

In the mid-1950s multi-tube space frames came into use, but as the 1960s opened Chapman was developing a backbone chassis for sports cars, and for a single-seater envisaged a backbone wide enough to accommodate a driver. The outcome was the monocoque 25. Its aluminium and steel chassis was jig-built with two side pontoons (which held fuel tanks) linked by the floor, fascia panel frame and front and rear bulkheads. The top had an unstressed plastics cover (hence this type of chassis was a semi-monocoque, or 'bath tub'), and the driver was laid back between the pontoons, to reduce frontal area.

The monocoque was not new to racing – there were precedents from the 1915 Cornelian Indy car through to the centre section of the Jaguar D type – but Chapman's interpretation was complete. It was more expensive than a space frame, but lighter and immensely rigid, and that allowed him to use a supple suspension that gave benefits in cornering. With the exception of Ferrari and Brabham, every other GP constructor was building monocoque cars by 1965, when Lotus was already introducing them for lesser categories; monocoque chassis became obligatory in GP racing in 1970, and had spread to track racing. There was an additional benefit in safety factors, and the 'survival cell' in modern materials meant that drivers have escaped serious injury in some lurid accidents.

Meanwhile, Jim Clark won five 1962 GPs in 25s, but component failures on the Lotus handed the championships to Hill and BRM in the final race of the year. In 1963 Clark won seven GPs, to take the Drivers' Championship while Lotus won the first of its seven Constructors' Championships. The 25 was still used in 1964, and its final tally was 14 Championship GP victories and 11 wins in non-title races.

The 33 was a development of the 25, with modifications to the monocoque and suspension to suit wider tyres, as well as in other details. In 1965 it gave Clark and Lotus the two titles again, with six GP victories, and the brilliant Scot drove 33s to win the 1967 Tasman Championship. Meanwhile, with Coventry Climax or BRM V8s enlarged as far as possible (to 2.1-litres), the 33s had to serve during the opening phase of the 3-litre GP Formula, predictably with little success, although in the type's last race with Team Lotus, Graham Hill placed a BRM-engined 33 second in the 1967 Monaco GP.

RIGHT
The 33 was a derivative of the 25, and its fatter tyres made it look much more solid. In this 1965 British GP grid shot, Clark is starting his 33 from pole, with Hill (BRM), Ginther (Honda) and Stewart (BRM) alongside him on the front row, and team mate Mike Spence in another 33 behind them.

BRM P261

Through its first and last phases, in the 1950s and 1970s, the BRM venture was hopeless, but in the 1960s it was a leading team and both Constructors' and Drivers' World Championships fell to it in 1962.

By the second year of the 1½-litre GP formula, BRM's fuel-injected 90 degree 1498 cc V8 was raceworthy, producing 184 bhp. It powered the neat space-frame P57, and drove through a five-speed BRM gearbox. For most of its existence, BRM shared with Ferrari the distinction of making all the main components on its cars, whereas most other GP entrants used bought-in items such as engines or gearboxes.

Graham Hill drove P57s to win four GPs in 1962, heading a team 1-2 in the Italian race, and took his first drivers' title. He won just two GPs in 1963, the U.S. race with a P61. The team had to make up ground lost to Colin Chapman's monocoque Lotus 25 that year, and via the P61 (designed by Tony Rudd, with a stressed-skin main body and tubular-frame engine bay) developed the monocoque P261 for 1964-65. For the second of those years, the V8 produced 212 bhp at the then-high speed of 11500 rpm, and there was a six-speed gearbox.

In 1964 Hill once again won the Monaco and U.S. Grands Prix, and was in contention for the World Championship through to its final race – the reliability of these cars was outstanding. For 1965 he was joined by Jackie Stewart, who was to score his first GP victory in Italy; Graham drove an astonishing race to complete a hat trick at Monaco, and for the third time coupled that with a victory in the U.S. Grand Prix at Watkins Glen.

With the V8 enlarged to 1970 cc the P261s had to be used in the opening races of the 3-litre GP Formula in 1966, and Stewart drove one to score BRM's fourth consecutive victory at Monaco, and these cars continued into 1967 in Tasman racing.

BRM was a successful team in the 1960s, especially with its 1½-litre cars. Graham Hill is driving this P261, turning into the Gasworks hairpin at Monaco in 1965.

Lotus Indianapolis Cars

In 1962 American driver Dan Gurney persuaded Lotus chief Colin Chapman to watch the Indianapolis 500, where save for Cooper's exploratory entry in 1961, technical stagnation had set in. At the same time, Ford was developing a 'performance' image, and this was to focus on two main objectives, the Le Mans 24-hour Race and the 500. Once Ford and Lotus came together the days of the traditional Indianapolis roadster were numbered.

The track racing Lotus 29 followed the innovative F1 25, with a longer wheelbase to comply with USAC regulations and asymmetrical suspension for the left-only turns of the Speedway. Naturally, components such as the suspension were beefier. The engine was a 4.2-litre derivative of the Fairlane pushrod ohv 90 degree V8, giving some 370 bhp on gasoline. The nitro-methane-fuelled Offenhauser engine that ruled track racing at the time gave just over 400 bhp. The average roadster weight was 1680 lb, the Lotus weighed about 1350 lb and its V8 needed less fuel.

The general opinion was that Clark and Lotus should have won the 500 at their first attempt. Clark was always within striking distance of the leader of that 1963 race, but Lotus pit work was poor and as the leading car in the closing phase was dropping oil, it was assumed that the chief steward would call it in. He did not. Parnelli Jones in that Watson Offy won by 19 seconds. Clark was second, Gurney seventh in the other Lotus, and later they were first and third in a 200-mile race at Milwaukee.

Lotus was back in 1964 with the 34, an improved car with a dohc Ford V8 giving 410 bhp, but tyre failures let them down. The 38 for 1965 was a new design, with a full monocoque, greater fuel capacity and the Ford V8 adapted to burn alcohol fuel, output rising to 500 bhp.

Jim Clark led all but 10 of the 200 laps of the 1964 500 in a 38, and won at 150.68 mph. Parnelli Jones in a 34 was second, Al Miller's 29 was fourth, and Bobby Johns' 38 was seventh. Lotus also won at Trenton and Milwaukee.

All but one of the cars in the 1966 Indianapolis 500 were rear-engined, Lotus ran the 38s again, and Clark was second behind Graham Hill's Lola. In 1967 they were Lotus team mates, but Clark in a 38 and Hill in the 42 both retired from the 500.

That race had seen the debut of the STP-Paxton turbocar, an odd device with its engine alongside the cockpit, which seemed to be heading for victory when a minor gearbox fault put it out of contention. The rules were hastily revised to curb gas turbine cars, but Andy Granatelli of STP and Chapman felt that one could still win the 500, and they came together for 1968.

The Lotus 56 was a startling wedge car, with a modified Pratt & Whitney industrial gas turbine giving perhaps 480 bhp, whereas 550 bhp had been possible before the restrictions were applied. A Ferguson four-wheel drive system was used.

A test accident in one of these cars cost the life of Mike Spence, but the red Lotus dominated the grid, and Jo Leonard seemed to be heading for victory when the engine died with nine laps to go (a fuel pump drive failed). The 56s were classified 12th (Leonard) 13th (Pollard) and 19th (Hill). USAC imposed further restrictions which made further turbine attempts pointless (one 56 was modified with a turbocharged Offenhauser). Lotus adapted a car as the 56B for GP racing in 1971. Lotus' final Indianapolis effort came in 1969 with the complex and inelegant 64, with a turbocharged 2.6-litre Ford V8 and four-wheel drive, but this type never started a race.

BELOW
The off-set suspension common on track-racing cars into the 1960s shows on this 38.

BELOW RIGHT
Two of the 38's predecessors were on the front row of the 1964 Indianapolis line-up – Clark in a 34 on pole nearest the camera, and Marshman in a 29 'Firechief Special' in the centre. The third car is Ward's Offenhauser-engined Watson, looking clumsy beside the Lotus pair.

Brabham-Repco

Jack Brabham in his BT19, a modest car which reaped a rich reward. There is some very artistic pipe bending in those exhausts!

Jack Brabham's first Grand Prix car, BT3, was built in 1962 and his first to win was the BT7, driven by Dan Gurney in the 1964 French race. For the new 3-litre formula in 1966 his partner and designer Ron Tauranac contrived the BT19, adapting a chassis intended for earlier use to take a Repco V8, based on an Oldsmobile engine. The simple and one-off BT19 earned its place in history when Brabham won the 1966 French GP with it – the first time a driver had won a championship race in a car bearing his own name.

The straightforward space frame, and suspension members outboard in the airstream, ignored Formula 1 trends. In Australia, Phil Irving and Repco engineer Frank Hallam, had already started work on a racing version of the V8, and they developed a 2996 cc unit. This sohc engine was hardly fashionable, and its initial claimed output of less than 300 bhp seemed almost hopeless when Ferrari rated its 3-litre V12 at 360 bhp.

After his historic victory at Reims, Jack Brabham went on to win the next three GPs (British, Dutch and German), to take his third drivers' title and win the Constructors' Championship for Brabham-Repco in its first year. The mildly improved BT20 was raced by Denny Hulme in 1966 and early 1967, when he won at Monaco with it.

The BT24 on similar lines came in 1967, Brabham driving it to win two GPs, while Hulme added the German GP to his Monaco victory and with points scored in good placings, beat Jack Brabham to the drivers' title, while the marques title fell to Brabham for the second time. Then the Brabham-Repco partnership fell apart, as a more complex new engine proved unreliable.

Eagle T1G

Americans Dan Gurney and Carroll Shelby formed All-American Racers in 1965, with Goodyear backing to break Firestone's run of success at Indianapolis. Shelby soon left, and Gurney set up a parallel GP operation in England under the title Anglo-American Racers. The AAR cars were to be named Eagles.

Len Terry was engaged to design a dual-purpose car, and for GP racing a V12 designed by Aubrey Woods was put in hand by Weslake, while the first USAC cars were to have Ford V8s. Terry used a light alloy monocoque and conventional GP suspension in a car resembling the Lotus 38, which he had executed for Chapman.

The V12 was late, and through to the summer of 1966 Gurney built up team experience using Coventry Climax 2.75-litre engines (scoring the first championship points for Eagle with a fifth place in the French GP). When the 2997 cc 60 degree V12 finally arrived, it was rated at 364 bhp, and it gave 410 bhp early in 1967.

There were teething problems, the car was overweight, and the V12 was inconsistent, but Gurney won the non-championship Race of Champions in 1967. His great moment came in June, when he won the Belgian GP at 145.98 mph. After that there were too many disappointments, Gurney raced an F1 Eagle for the last time in the 1968 Italian GP.

Eagle was to make a stronger impact at Indianapolis, Hulme taking fourth place in one of the 1967 cars (Gurney retired, but later won a Riverside race). Gurney and Hulme were second and fourth in Ford-powered cars in 1968, while Bobby Unser won in a later Offenhauser-powered car.

The beak nose was a distinctive feature of the blue and white Eagle GP cars, as were the six-spoke cast magnesium wheels and the exhausts of the V12. This T1G is being driven by Dan Gurney. The T1G had a distinctive 'beak' nose, set off by its blue and white American racing colours. This early car, at Reims in 1966, has a Coventry Climax four-cylinder engine, which was not outstandingly powerful but did make for a clear rear end.

Gurney scored the first victory for Eagle on a dull day at Brands Hatch early in 1967, when he won the non-championship Race of Champions. Three months later Gurney drove an Eagle to victory in the Belgian GP, which save for the minor point that the car was 'Made in Britain' was the first Grand Prix win for an American car – let alone an American car/driver combination – since Murphy won the French race in a Duesenberg in 1921.

Overall the T1G was a handsome car, and in detail the finish was outstanding. In racing it was let down by its weight and inconsistent V12s, and in 1967 Dan Gurney abandoned Grand Prix racing, to enjoy considerable success in the U.S.A. in the 1970s before he had to turn away from single-seaters.

Lotus 49

This was a key car of the 3-litre GP Formula, introduced in 1966. It was in the front line for four years and was designed for the Ford-Cosworth DFV engine that was to power the winning cars in 154 Grands Prix and lead to other outstanding engines, including turbo track racing units. It was also central to the 'wings' episode.

Colin Chapman was instrumental in bringing together Keith Duckworth of Cosworth and Ford's Harley Copp and Walter Hayes. Their

company was to underwrite the V8 that became known as the DFV. Chapman reckoned that one untried major component would be enough, so Maurice Phillipe's 49 design was straightforward, unusual only in that the engine was a load-bearing member, bolted to the bulkhead behind the cockpit and with the rear suspension sub-frame bolted to it. There were to be many changes – for example, ZF transmission gave way to Hewland gearboxes in 1968. At the early stage, the compact 2993 cc V8 was rated at 408 bhp, with fierce power curve characteristics; by the end of the 49's life, it gave some 430 bhp.

The car won first time out, driven by Jim Clark in the 1967 Dutch GP, and he went on to win the British, U.S. and Mexican GPs; although his team mate, Graham Hill, led GPs, he was out of luck. Clark won the opening GP in 1968, then he was killed in a minor German race. Graham rallied the team by winning the next races, in Spain and Monaco, and late in the year he won the Mexican GP in a 49B to clinch the Drivers' Championship. Meanwhile in mid-season, Swiss Jo Siffert had driven Walker's dark blue 49B to win the British GP – the last Grand Prix victory for a private entrant.

The Team Lotus cars Hill and Oliver drove in 1968 were in the bright colours of Player's Gold Leaf cigarette brand, for Chapman had turned to full commercial sponsorship as 'traditional' racing support faded and costs escalated. Soon the 49s carried strut-mounted aerofoils, or 'wings', which generated download to improve traction – and also increased stresses. In 1969 the rear wings on the two 49Bs in the Spanish GP failed, leading to spectacular accidents and clinching arguments against these devices, which were banned.

The high point in the 49's third season came at Monaco, where Graham Hill scored his fifth victory in the classic street race. Late in the year his team mate Jochen Rindt scored his maiden GP victory – which many considered overdue – in the U.S. race at Watkins Glen, where Hill crashed very heavily. Against expectations, he was to recover to race Rob Walker's Lotus 49 and 72, although he never regained leading status.

LEFT
The 49 was to undergo several transformations while it was a Team Lotus front-line car from 1967 until 1970. In 1968, the 49 still had an exposed DFV, but there were no aerofoils on the 49s run in the 1967 Dutch GP, the tyres are wider and the roll-over bar is substantial, there is top ducting from the radiators, and of course Lotus' green and yellow colours have gone. The driver in this Monza pit shot is Mario Andretti.

BELOW
Jim Clark scored a convincing debut victory with a 49 in the 1967 Dutch GP. Following him in that race is Denny Hulme, in a Brabham.

As its intended replacements disappointed, or in the case of the 72 ran late, the 49 had to be reworked to 'C' specification for 1970, and one more GP fell to it, at Monaco, driven by Rindt. It was still valuable, for example when future World Champion Emerson Fittipaldi, drove his first GP in a Gold Leaf Team Lotus 49C, at Brands Hatch. He had still been racing karts in Brazil when Clark scored the first of the 12 World Championship races that fell to the 49 – the simple design with its no-nonsense engine had extraordinary stamina.

Matra-Ford

The French Matra aerospace company become involved in the motor industry and motor racing almost accidentally, when as a creditor it took over the little René Bonnet specialist car company in 1964. At the end of the decade it became the first – and so far only – French constructor to win the GP Constructors' Championship.

Its 1969 success was largely due to the perceptive Ken Tyrrell, and to Jackie Stewart – Tyrrell had won the European Formula 2 Championship with Matras, Stewart and Jackie Ickx in 1967. He was impressed by Matra's GP chassis, but wanted to use the Cosworth DFV engine (Lotus' exclusive-use period ended in 1968), rather than the V12 that Matra was developing for a French government-backed 'all-French' car. The outcome was a Franco-British car, with components such as the DFV V8 and Hewland gearbox complementing the excellent monocoque chassis and suspension in the MS10.

After a hesitant start, Stewart drove the light blue MS10 to win the Dutch GP in 1968, following that with an epic win in the cloud- and rain-enveloped German GP and a late-season victory in the U.S. Grand Prix. Designer Bernard Boyer incorporated substantial improvements in the MS80 for 1969, and Stewart made full use of this car's outstanding qualities by winning the Spanish, Dutch, French, British and Italian GPs, taking the drivers' title for himself and the constructors' title for Matra. Then the regulations changed and the MS80 was obsolete after one season.

By 1970 Matra had associations with Simca that ruled out another car with 'Ford' on its engine's cam covers; its own 'all-Matra' effort succeeded in sports-car racing, but never in the Grands Prix although the Ligier team won three GPs with Matra engines.

BELOW
Jackie Stewart drove a brilliant race in foul conditions to win the 1968 German GP by more than four minutes. His MS10 carried Matra's earliest aerofoils, a relatively modest rear wing and balancing tabs at the nose.

RIGHT
In 1969 the Matra MS80 had an integrated rear aerofoil and little fences on the nose. This shot of Stewart at Silverstone also shows the 'coke-bottle' body lines and the fairings over the front suspension pivot points.

Tyrrell 001-006

To continue in Grand Prix racing once the Matras his team had used so successfully were no longer eligible, Ken Tyrrell had to build his own cars. He started the 1970 season with March 701s, but before Jackie Stewart had raced one of these for the first time, Tyrrell had commissioned Derek Gardner to design the first Tyrrell car, to be built in great secrecy. That 001 was deliberately simple, and a more refined version came for 1971, numbered 002-004. In 1973 there were 005 and three cars numbered 006 – Tyrrell at last started to use type numbers rather than individual chassis numbers. At the end of that year, when François Cevert was fatally injured in practice for the U.S. Grand Prix, and Stewart retired, the first Tyrrells had won 16 GPs – in the next 20 years there were to be just 7 more victories.

Gardner worked on that first design at his home, and the dark blue car was clean and simple, with an open-topped monocoque and Cosworth DFV engine used as a stressed chassis member. In plan it had bulging sides in the 'coke-bottle' style of the Matra MS80, but the most distinctive outward feature was a semi-wedge nose with a broad aerofoil above the radiator intake.

Stewart drove 001 in four late-1970 races; it failed to finish in any, for trivial reasons, but its potential was demonstrated, and that justified the cost of around two-and-a-half times that of one of the March cars, used early in the season.

The two new cars for 1971 had improved chassis, suspension and brakes, and by mid-season had 'air boxes' above the engine, intended to feed air straight to the induction trumpets of the V8. Soon there were bluff nose cones, to clean airflow over the front wheels and kill lift. 004 was completed on these lines for 1972.

Stewart won six GPs in 1971, with his promising young team mate François Cevert twice following him past the chequered flag. The Scot became World Champion; remarkably, Tyrrell won the Constructors' Championship with more than twice as many points as the runner-up, in his first full season as a constructor! Then Stewart used 003 to win two 1972 GPs.

The second-generation Tyrrell cars, 005 and 006 for 1972-73 were more angular, with slab-sided monocoques, shorter and lower, with improved weight distribution and aerodynamics, and were light and manoeuvrable. At first there were little side intakes for oil radiators, then as the cars were revised to meet 'deformable structure' safety regulations, there were larger intakes aligned with the back of the cockpit for water radiators, while the oil radiators were moved to the nose. Inboard brakes were tried all round, but at a slight cost in unsprung weight, they were moved outboard at the front.

In 1973 Jackie Stewart raised his tally of GP victories to 27, then a record – in gaining the Drivers' Championship for the third time, the brilliant Scot won in South Africa, Belgium, Monaco, Holland and Germany. As he retired, Ken Tyrrell had to restructure his team and his two new drivers, Scheckter and Depailler, started the 1974 season with the existing cars.

ABOVE
Jackie Stewart and Ken Tyrrell pose with the first Tyrrell Grand Prix car, in the late summer of 1970.

BELOW LEFT
Tyrrell 003 was a workmanlike car, driven by Stewart in 1971 (here in the U.S. Grand Prix).

BELOW RIGHT
The Tyrrell pair, Stewart and Cevert, driving two of the 006 cars in the 1973 Swedish GP, when these were in their final form, with hip water radiators and one of the best-looking air boxes.

McLaren M16

McLaren's first Indianapolis foray came in 1970, when the team was dominant in the CanAm sports-racing series, and in contrast the '500' venture was hardly successful – Carl Williams placed an M15 ninth, but to set against that Denny Hulme had a nasty fire accident before the race, and immediately after it Bruce McLaren died in a CanAm car test accident. The team pulled together, designer Gordon Coppuck built on experience, and early in 1971 the wedge-bodied M16 was unveiled.

The wedge nose was clean as hip radiators were used, and was part of an aerodynamic package that drew on GP experience with 'wings' and the knowledge that wedge lines would be ideal for sustained high-speed running on an oval. The power unit was the 2.65-litre turbocharged Offenhauser four-cylinder engine, based on an early-1930s design and giving some 700 bhp in the early 1970s; it drove through a three-speed Hewland gearbox.

In an M16 run by the Penske team, Mark Donohue became the first driver to lap the Speedway in less than 50 seconds, before qualification. He led the 1971 500, retired, saw Peter Revson finish second in a works M16, and five weeks later won the Pocono 500. Donohue then posted McLaren's first Indianapolis victory with an updated Penske M16B in 1972. The sleeker 1973 M16C had the benefit of some feedback from the M23 GP car, that in turn had followed the lines of the original M16.

That season was not outstanding, but in 1974 the Indianapolis 500 again fell to a McLaren, the M16C/D driven by Johnny Rutherford, with David Hobbs in the other works car placing fifth.

The design was reworked as the longer and sleeker M16E for 1975 by John Barnard. That year Rutherford was second in the 500, and he was to win at Indianapolis again, driving an M16E to victory in the rain-shortened (255 miles) 1976 race.

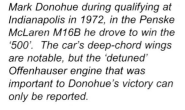

Mark Donohue during qualifying at Indianapolis in 1972, in the Penske McLaren M16B he drove to win the '500'. The car's deep-chord wings are notable, but the 'detuned' Offenhauser engine that was important to Donohue's victory can only be reported.

LEFT
Rutherford posing with the winning M16E in 1976.

BELOW
Peter Revson being waved out of the pits at Indianapolis in 1971. From this angle the 'hip radiator' of his orange works M16A is prominent, as is the single high-mounted rear-view mirror.

LEFT
Johnny Rutherford in a works M16C in 1973. This variant has an odd engine cover merging into the rear wing, and the radiator shrouds have been revised. Rutherford took pole, but was only ninth in the race.

Lotus 72

RIGHT
A Lotus 72 in its earliest form, driven by Jochen Rindt. The clean nose, with its little 'chimneys' for the inboard brakes' hot air, shows well, as does the three-tier rear aerofoil.

BELOW
Wedge lines of the 72 show in this 1972 shot of Fittipaldi at Silverstone, as do aerodynamic changes and an odd 'air box' over the engine.

Lotus' gas turbine 56B and four-wheel drive 63, both Grand Prix spin-offs from Indianapolis projects, showed little promise, and the true successor to the 49 was the innovative 72.

By 1971 the DFV was widely used, so Colin Chapman looked for other advantages. The 72 had wedge profile lines for aerodynamic efficiency, and to that end 'hip' radiators aligned with the back of the cockpit were used instead of nose radiators. There was torsion bar suspension to exploit the then-new soft compound tyres, and inboard brakes to keep heat away from them as well as reduce unsprung weight. Through the car's long career (72 to 72F) there were neat nose aerofoils and a variety of large rear wings, and while the car was still fairly new, the first of the engine air boxes that were to feature on many racing cars were used. The DFV engine and Hewland gearbox seemed almost commonplace.

Teething troubles were perhaps inevitable, but by mid-1970 the car was raceworthy, and Jochen Rindt won the Dutch, French, British and German GPs in succession. Then he was fatally injured in practice for the Italian GP – Fittipaldi's win in the U.S. race (his first GP victory) then ensured that Rindt became the sport's first posthumous champion.

The 1971 season was largely barren, but in 1972 Fittipaldi won five GPs, taking the drivers' title and the Constructors' Championship for Lotus. Lotus' title was held in 1973, but as Fittipaldi won three races and Ronnie Peterson four they were beaten to the individual title by Jackie Stewart. Peterson won another three GPs in 1974. In 1975 the 72 was outclassed, at last, but its record of 20 GP victories stood until 1986.

Ferrari 312T

In the mid-1970s Ferrari was on top of the world again, as its Grand Prix team was the first to win three consecutive Constructors' Championships – a feat unmatched until McLaren took the title in 1988-91, and one which must have particularly pleased Enzo Ferrari. He had taken action to halt the slide in fortunes in 1972-73; the pointless sports-racing programme was abandoned, Mauro Forghieri was reinstated as chief engineer – a position which really did mean technical supremo, from design to supervision at race meetings – and Luca de Montezemolo was appointed team manager. Results came in 1974, as Niki Lauda and Clay Regazzoni won three championship races with the 312B3.

There was still great potential in the 12-cylinder engine (a 'boxer' or 'flat' unit, with its two banks of cylinders at 180 degrees) and in 2992 cc form in 1975 it gave up to 485 bhp, some 20 bhp more than the rival Cosworth DFV at little cost in weight. As usual in Ferrari designations, the '3' signified 3-litres and '12' the number of cylinders; 'T' was added for *trasversale*, for the transverse gearbox which was installed with the input turned through 90 degrees to the fore-and-aft line. The engine was low and well forward in the chassis, keeping the centre of gravity low and

with its mass towards the centre, making for a very nimble car.

There was a monocoque hull and the sculpted side pods contained radiators, while the tall air box above the engine was nicely integrated into the overall design. The 312T looked even better in its 1976 (312T2) form, when air boxes had been banned and engine air was neatly channelled alongside the cockpit. The body lines became more angular in 1978 (312T3), when there were more changes 'under the skin'.

Intensive work at Ferrari's Fiorano track meant that the team and lead driver Lauda were thoroughly prepared for each GP, and the Austrian delivered the goods in 1975 with five victories (and took the drivers' title), while Regazzoni won the Italian GP. Ferrari was Champion Constructor by a wide margin.

The next year the points gap was narrower, largely because the second half of the season was confused after Lauda's fiery accident at the Nürburgring. Before the 312T2 came, he had won two of the first three races, Regga the other. Then with the new car, and up to 500 bhp,

Lauda won two more GPs before that German race.

There was a generous 32-point gap between Ferrari and championship runner-up Lotus in 1977. Lauda won three GPs and the Drivers' Championship, while Carlos Reutemann won in Brazil. Later that year Gilles Villeneuve drove his first races for Ferrari, and on his home circuit at Montreal in 1978 scored his first GP victory. Reutemann won three GPs.

That year Lotus won the Constructors' Championship, and Ferrari had to turn to ground effects, with skirts on the 312T3 late in the year. Ground effects were part of the 1979-80 312T4-T5 make-up, despite problems imposed by the cylinder heads of the flat-12. In 1979 all was well – there were six GP victories, Jody Scheckter and Villeneuve were clearly first and second on the drivers' points table, and Ferrari regained the champion team position. That made the complete failure in 1980 surprising – Ferrari did not even achieve a double figure points score, in a sad end to the story of the illustrious flat-12 Grand Prix cars.

LEFT
As the 312T5, the 1980 Ferrari was a very different car, and in the final year for the 312 series a miserably uncompetitive one, too. This 1980 Dutch GP shot shows the curious nose bodywork and the skirts that were an essential part of a 'ground effects' car. The driver is Jody Scheckter.

McLaren M23

Gordon Coppuck's first Grand Prix car design was outstandingly successful. The M23 served the McLaren team for four years, with a harvest of 16 Championship GP victories, a constructors' title and drivers' championships for Emerson Fittipaldi and James Hunt. And after that, the M23s had long second-level careers.

Coppuck was able to draw on the M16 Indianapolis car and use elements such as the suspension from the GP M19, as well as the depth of practical experience in the team. The car conformed to the then-new 'deformable structure' requirements, introduced with driver safety in mind, having a narrow monocoque and integral side pods which housed radiators and contributed to stiffness. The engine was almost inevitably the Cosworth DFV, giving some 465 bhp by 1976, when it drove through a six-speed gearbox.

Denny Hulme put an M23 on pole for its first race, in South Africa in 1973, and later that year won the Swedish GP in the Yardley-liveried car, while his team mate Peter Revson won in Britain and Canada.

There was a change to Texaco-Marlboro colours for 1974 (with a single 'Yardleymac' for Mike Hailwood); Hulme and Fittipaldi won four GPs, and with four major USAC victories for M16s to add to the two world titles, that was a golden year for McLaren. In 1975 there were revisions to solve handling problems, and just three GP wins (two for Fittipaldi, one for Jochen Mass).

So to the tense 1976 season, when James Hunt won the title by just one point in the last race, having previously won six GPs in the Marlboro-McLarens and been disqualified from another in a season-long duel with Niki Lauda.

Hunt's M23 in the 1976 British GP wears the Marlboro colours that have been a constant McLaren feature since 1974, in racing's longest team/sponsor partnership.

Penske PC6

Roger Penske was a prominent amateur racing driver in the 1960s, who turned entrant and then became a constructor in the 1970s. With driver Mark Donohue he had entered USAC racing in 1969, when Donohue placed Penske's Lola seventh in their Indianapolis debut, then won with the team's McLaren in 1972, and in the early 1970s Penske entered Formula 1. Graham McRae's plant at Poole in Dorset was acquired, and in the mid-1990s is still Penske's design and build base. The PC1 GP car appeared in 1974; John Watson drove a PC4 to score Penske's only GP win in Austria in 1976, before the team abandoned Formula 1 and concentrated on U.S. racing again.

In 1977 Tom Sneva won the USAC Citicorp championship with Penske's McLaren M24, and for 1978 Geoff Ferris designed Penske's first Indianapolis car, the PC6. This was a conventional single-seater, sleek and carefully engineered, and powered by the 2.6-litre Cosworth DFX turbocharged V8 that was taking over USAC racing (it had been used in Al Unser's Parnelli that won three 1976 races, and in 1978 was used in four types of chassis that won all but five of the races in that last purely USAC season).

The PC6 was very reliable, and that factor gained the championship for Tom Sneva, for quite remarkably he failed to win a single race – he was second six times, and third four times. His Penske team mate Rick Mears, won three races, and the pair were 1-2 in a USAC race at Brands Hatch.

The PC7 was effectively a 'ground effects' version of PC6 for 1979. However, Penske ran a PC6 for Mears at Indianapolis, and he won the '500' with it, while Johncock won two races in a PC6 entered by Patrick Racing, before the PC7s started to win regularly.

Lotus 79

Team Lotus fortunes slumped in the mid-1970s and, typically, Colin Chapman looked to an original means to restore them in the 'wing car', developed by a Lotus project group. Other designers had hesitantly approached the concept, but then backed away, but the Lotus R&D team persevered in its investigation into using the airflow under a car, as well as airflow loadings on aerofoils pressing it down onto the road. Signs of their work to control under-car airflow came in the 77 in the second half of 1977 (at the end of that year, Mario Andretti drove a 77 to victory in the Japanese GP).

The full results of research were seen in the 78. This had the widely-used DFV engine and Hewland gearbox, and much that was new. The slim monocoque was flanked by wide side pods containing radiators and fuel tanks, and an 'inverted wing section', while the outer bottom edges were sealed to the track to control the airflow. The front track was as wide as possible to give good grip, with suspension members tucked out of the way to make for smooth airflow to the pods. Sucking the car to the track was all-important.

With a characteristically apt phrase, Mario Andretti described Lotus wing car roadholding as 'painted to the road', and in 1977 he won four GPs in 78s, and Gunnar Nilsson took one; no other driver won as many GPs as Andretti, no team as many as Lotus, but the points scoring system meant that world titles went elsewhere. In 1978 Andretti and Ronnie Peterson each won a GP in a 78, before the 79 was introduced.

The 79 was more than a refined 78, and the download generated was so great that after first tests a stronger monocoque had to be used. There was still a radiator in each side pod (water on the right, oil on the left), but the fuel was in a cell between cockpit and engine, thus clearing the pods while keeping this changing load at the centre of gravity, to maintain constant handling. The rear suspension was kept out of the airflow on the 79.

This proved to be the outstanding car of 1978, reliable as well as fast on any given circuit. Andretti won four more GPs, and with the points scored early in the year with a 78, was World Champion by a wide margin. Peterson won once in a 79, was loyally second four times, before his fatal accident at Monza. Stand-in driver Jean-Pierre Jarier then underlined the qualities of the car, as he took pole for his second race in it, at Montreal.

However, other teams quickly caught up, and 79 performances were no more than average early in 1979. Not for the first time, Chapman tried to go too far with the next GP Lotus. The 80 had side pods curved inside the rear wheels, even had little skirts under the nose, but track behaviour was unpredictable and the 80 was run in only three races. The 81 incorporated much 79 technology, but was no more than modestly successful.

The racing world had to follow a Lotus initiative once again, as ' ground effects' spread through Formula 1, into the secondary categories, to track racing and to sports cars.

OPPOSITE
The Lotus 78 had a slim monocoque and broad side pods, containing water radiators. 'Ground effects' airflow passed through these. The small nose radiator is the oil cooler.

LEFT
The Lotus 79 was attractive from any angle, and was the outstanding car of 1978. The drivers of this pair are Mario Andretti and Ronnie Peterson.

Renault Turbo Cars

Renault introduced turbocharged engines to the Grands Prix in 1977, and sparked a costly power race which was to be curbed before turbos were banned in 1989. Meanwhile, the smart French cars enjoyed mixed fortunes, winning 15 Grands Prix from 123 races entered.

A turbocharger is a compressor to boost the fuel-air mixture forced into an engine, to increase power output; its small turbine is rotated by exhaust gas, and it performs a similar function to a supercharger, but without using mechanical power. It is also light and compact, but it rotates at very high speeds and in heat; intercoolers were needed with racing engines, adding bulk and weight. Turbos had long been used on aero engines and were normal in track racing before Renault brought them to road racing on sports cars, six years before its first turbo GP car, RS01, first raced (at Silverstone in 1977).

RS01 was a conventional design by André de

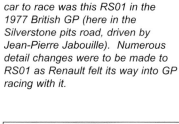

The first turbocharged Grand Prix car to race was this RS01 in the 1977 British GP (here in the Silverstone pits road, driven by Jean-Pierre Jabouille). Numerous detail changes were to be made to RS01 as Renault felt its way into GP racing with it.

Cortanze, but interest focused on its EFI 90-degree V6 engine, with its single Garrett turbocharger. Under the GP regulations, it was subject to an 'equivalency factor' of 2:1, which on first showings seemed about right – the 500 bhp rating of this 1.5-litre turbo unit was similar to that for the 3-litre engines in other cars. RS01 was not competitive – it failed to finish in five starts in 1977, and finished only 5 times in 14 starts in 1978. But Renault persevered, battling to overcome throttle lag and problems such as loss of power caused by overheating.

RS10 for 1979 was a slender ground effects car, and its engine with twin KKK turbos gave 520 bhp. Unreliability still dogged the team, but it achieved a near-perfect result in the all-important French GP, when Jabouille and Arnoux were first and third.

By 1980 Renault was a leading GP team. That year's car was the RE20, with sleeker lines,

but little more power; the team won three GPs, and newcomer Alain Prost repeated that score with the RE30 in 1981. The engine was still modestly rated, at 540 bhp, but other turbos were beginning to appear and that was to force the development pace – for 1983 the Renault was to have larger turbos and water injection, and output was up to 650 bhp.

Meanwhile, three more GPs had fallen to the RE30B in 1982, when the chassis was becoming outmoded and the retirement rate approached 60 per cent. Inconsistency dogged the RE40 in 1983, when Prost won four GPs, but lost out to Brabham driver Piquet in the championship. The little Frenchman was made a scapegoat and was sacked.

'Blame the pilot' might have soothed the board of a national company, but the 1984 season proved it fallacious, for Renault cars were to win no more Grands Prix. The RE50 of 1984 had 750 bhp, but it had fuel consumption problems on one hand and suspect front suspension on the other, and seemed accident-prone. The RE60 had power in abundance, with two new engines available – EF4 rated at 760 bhp or EF15 giving 810 bhp in race trim and up to 1000 bhp available with turbo boost increased for qualifying, when stamina was not essential.

Neither car was a winner, although by 1985 Lotus was winning races with Renault 'customer' turbo engines. The French team had ushered in an era of over-powerful cars, which sometimes looked spectacular (and were prone to engine compartment blazes), and cost teams fortunes. They set records, introduced little new technology, and now seem to be recalled with little affection.

Williams-Ford

In 1977 Frank Williams at last secured backing to build his own GP cars, and exploit the talents of designer Patrick Head. Their FW06 was one of the most promising conventional DFV-powered cars in 1978, but that year the benefits of ground effects in helping to close the performance gap to the powerful Ferrari and Renault engines were shown by Lotus.

Williams adopted ground effects in the FW07, laid out by Head with Neil Oatley, then developed with Frank Dernie. It inevitably followed the Lotus 79 in its broad outline, with side pods housing radiators and ground-effects aerofoils, sealed to the track with sliding skirts, and the fuel cell was on the centre line behind the cockpit.

The FW07 was fast from the outset, and at Silverstone Clay Regazzoni scored Williams' first Grand Prix victory with a commanding drive. Alan Jones then headed a Williams 1-2 in

Germany, and won in Austria, Holland and Canada. Williams was set to enter the 1980s as a major team.

In its first 'B' form the FW07 showed that undercar aerodynamics were still being explored, increased downforce leading to instability known by the self-explanatory term 'porpoising'. That cured, Jones and Carlos Reutemann were first and third in the Drivers' Championship, winning six GPs, and Williams was Champion Constructor for the first time. The second title was gained with the FW07C in 1981, when four GPs fell to Jones and Reutemann.

The FW08 which followed was on similar but more compact lines, and although Keke Rosberg drove it to take the 1982 Drivers' Championship, he won only two GPs with it, one being in 1983. That brought Williams' score of championship GP victories with Cosworth-powered cars to 17, all but two falling to FW07s.

The FW07 was the most elegant car of 1979, and in 'B' form it was the most successful car of 1980. Alan Jones is the driver, in his championship year, and his car shows off compact lines, low engine deck for optimum airflow to the rear wing, and details such as the 'ground effects' skirts.

Brabham-BMW

Brabham was a leading constructor as the 1980s opened and a faction within BMW gained broad support for an entry into racing's premier category, and initiated a turbocharged engine project. The two companies came together in the summer of 1980, and a BMW-powered Brabham first raced in 1982.

The BT50 followed the broad lines of Brabham's successful Cosworth-engined BT49, a little longer, bulkier and heavier. BMW designer Paul Rosche used the standard production four-cylinder iron block with an aluminium cylinder head that had been developed for Formula 2, adding a KKK turbocharger in an engine designated M12/13 (it associated with BMW's 'M-Power' image). This 1499 cc engine delivered some 570 bhp in its first racing season, but development had been agonizing, with many failures and other problems from injection to ignition.

Brabham started racing these engines in 1982, and Nelson Piquet drove a BT50 to win the Canadian GP. There were only three other points-scoring finishes, but Brabham kept in the headlines as the team reintroduced fuel stops to GP racing.

For 1983 Gordon Murray designed the dramatic BT52, with slim hull and no side pods, as weight was concentrated at the rear, BMW contributed more reliability and power – 640 bhp in race trim, up to 750 bhp for qualifying. Piquet won the Brazilian, Italian and European GPs, and the Drivers' Championship, while Patrese won in South Africa.

That was the Brabham-BMW high point, although with 850 bhp engines in the BT53 Piquet won two championship races in 1984. There was just one win for the 1985 BT54, and that was the last ever GP victory for a Brabham.

With its slim body, cockpit set well back, and prominent radiators alongside its BMW engine, the BT52 was unlike other cars on the 1983 GP grids. Turbo power meant that large wings could be used. The front suspension shows the care taken to minimize interference with the airflow.

McLaren-TAG

At the end of the 1970s, McLaren was a constructor in decline, but in 1980 a partnership with Project 4 injected new life; very soon it amounted to a take-over, with Ron Dennis and designer John Barnard of Project 4 in the leading roles. Their first new car introduced a fundamental development, the use of carbon-composites materials in the major structure – the monocoque chassis – as well as in appendages such as aerofoils, and soon McLaren had an exclusive turbo engine arrangement. Incidentally, the McLaren designation sequence was discarded for McLaren/Project 4 (MP4) numbers.

Barnard enlisted aerospace expertise in developing the carbon-composite moulded monocoque, and the first were made by Hercules in the U.S.A. This technology was costly, but made for structures that were extremely strong and rigid in most respects (there were some early misgivings about impact resistance). MP4/1 had a carbon fibre monocoque, and in other aspects was a clean-lined DFV-powered car.

John Watson scored the first victory for the revived team, in the 1981 British GP; Watson and Lauda won four GPs in 1982, and in 1983 Watson won the U.S.A.-West GP with an MP4/1C, a 'flat-bottom' car – the governing body had moved to curb clever designers' ways round the ground effects ban.

However, the Cosworth V8 was an interim power unit. Dennis had commissioned a turbocharged engine from Porsche, and obtained backing for it from Techniques d'Avant Garde

BELOW
With bodywork removed, the slender monocoque of the MP4/1E is obvious, and its manufacturer proclaimed. Soon every serious constructor would have an autoclave and be capable of producing carbon-composite chassis.

(TAG). This was a 1499 cc dohc 80 degree V6, with twin KKK turbochargers. In its early form it gave more than 600 bhp; that was soon increased, eventually to approach 1000 bhp. The engine unit was very compact, although its ancillaries took up space.

The MP4/1 was adapted for the first TAG engines, recording no finishes in seven starts in late-1983 races. That changed with the MP4/2, which was to serve McLaren through three seasons. It followed the lines of MP4/1, with a redesigned monocoque and side pods, refined aerodynamics and in 1985 revised suspension. There were to be detailed modifications through the car's A, B and C versions, and other modifications were called for when the fuel allowance for a Grand Prix was reduced.

Four cars were built for 1984, when Niki Lauda raced one for the whole season, and one was not raced at all. That made the score of 12 GP victories remarkable. Lauda won five, and

was World Champion; Prost won seven, and was runner-up in the Drivers' Championship. In the Constructors' Championship, McLaren scored 143½ points, while the second team on the table, Ferrari, scored a mere 57½. Such domination is rare.

In 1985 Prost won five GPs, and the drivers' title, and Lauda won just one race. McLaren was again champion team. Margins were narrower with MP4/2C in 1986, when Prost retained his title with four GP victories, plus the points from four second places and three thirds, but team mate Rosberg did not win a single GP and McLaren was second to Williams in the Constructors' Championship.

That situation was repeated in 1987. The MP4/3 designed by Steve Nichols was the last McLaren with the TAG engine, for the V6 was nearing the end of its development life. It was by no means outclassed, and Prost drove it to win three GPs. Then McLaren turned to Honda engines.

BELOW
The first turbo McLaren, driven by John Watson in practice for the European GP late in the year. The side pods are substantial and the drag of large rear wings was acceptable, for the downforce they provided.

LEFT
The continuity of line of the TAG-engined McLarens lasted through to 1986, in this MP4/2C. Then Nichols' MP4/3 design for 1987 appeared, with sleeker lines. The driver is Alain Prost.

March Indy Cars

In 1984, 30 of the 33 cars formed up for the start of the Indianapolis 500 were built by March, and every one of the 14 which finished was a March, heading the results list as a 'Pennzoil Z7', 'Master Mechanics' and 'Miller High Life' in the old tradition of 'Indianapolis Specials' named for the sponsors. The British company had built its first Indy car in 1980, and by the end of the decade its involvement had dwindled.

In the 1970s, March had become a major racing car manufacturer, with much success in secondary 'European' categories, but little in the Grands Prix. Its first production Indy car, 81C, showed that March could be a force in American racing – there were wins at Pocono, Milwaukee and Phoenix. Twenty 82Cs were built, then in 1983 Tom Sneva drove a Cosworth DFX-engined 83C to win the Indianapolis 500.

The 83C, Robin Herd's last design for the company he had jointly formed, evolved from 81C/82C, built round an aluminium honeycomb monocoque. In place of rocker-arm suspension, 83C had inboard coil springs and dampers with pull-rod activation, as part of the aerodynamic package. The Cosworth DFX drove through a March transverse gearbox that was acceptable for ovals – most entrants preferred a Hewland box for road circuits. Following the '500' there were half a dozen more 1983 victories, scored by Sneva, Fabi and Rahal.

March Indy car production was to peak with the 84C, with 47 being built. This was more compact, had better aerodynamics, and it was quick from the outset. There was a stunning Indianapolis result, with Rick Mears heading the 1-10, and four more first through fifth results in the 1984 CART/PPG series. The 85C and 86C had new monocoques, while there were only minor changes in 86C. Three more Indianapolis victories were highlights, these were scored by Danny Sullivan (1985), Bobby Rahal (1986) and Al Unser (1987). After that, the second place in the 500, scored by Fittipaldi with an Ilmor (Chevrolet) powered 88C, was almost an anti-climax, and 1989 results with the Porsche-engined 89P and the Alfa Romeo-engined 89CE were poor.

ABOVE
The 84C was chosen by most Indy Car entrants in 1984, and one outcome was a sensational Indianapolis result. The 1983 '500' victor Tom Sneva was sidelined by transmission failure in this 84C at Indianapolis, but was runner-up in the CART/PPG World Series.

LEFT
The March 83C was a highly rated 'customer car', which teams were to modify through the 1983 season, some almost to 'road' and 'track' versions. The Forsythe Racing 83C driven by Teo Fabi was a very strong contender (and at Pocono he became the first European driver to win a track 500 since Graham Hill won at Indianapolis in 1966).

Williams-Honda

In the 1960s, Honda's Grand Prix cars were only moderately successful, but the Japanese company returned late in 1983, supplying turbo engines to Williams in a partnership that was rewarding to both, with 18 Grand Prix victories and the 1986 and 1987 Constructors' Championships. Williams' need for a turbo engine had been underlined as it slipped from championship team in 1980-81 to fourth in 1982-83.

The Japanese RA163 80-degree V6, with twin IHI turbochargers, was powerful but not entirely driver-friendly, until development ironed out characteristics such as an 'on-off' power curve. It was first used in the FW09, one of the last front-line cars to have an aluminium monocoque. In the 1985 FW10, designer Patrick Head turned to a carbon-composite monocoque, and the rewards were seen as the car was developed, for three of its four GP victories were scored at the end of the season. Rosberg won twice, Mansell twice.

The FW11 was an even neater follow-on, and some of the cars built in the 1987 'B' form had a new computer-controlled active suspension system, with hydraulic jacks taking the place of normal dampers. The aims were to reduce pitch and give a constant ride height through a race. The Honda engine was developed in terms of fuel-efficiency as well as power output, because the fuel allowance for a race had been reduced to 195 litres (48.4 gallons).

In 1986 Nelson Piquet won four GPs, but was upstaged by Nigel Mansell, who won five, but lost out in the title race when a rear tyre failed. Piquet was champion in 1987 when he won only three GPs, but was second in seven GPs, piling up more points than Mansell, despite the British driver's six GP victories.

Honda unilaterally annulled the final year of its contract, dealing Williams a heavy blow as it set up an association with McLaren for 1988, which became Williams' worst season since 1978.

McLaren-Honda

RIGHT
Alain Prost on the streets of Phoenix, on his way to a U.S. Grand Prix victory in 1989. The large side pods of the MP4/5 are prominent, as are the fairings for the front suspension mountings.

BELOW
McLaren took over the leading role from Williams – the MP4/4 may not have been the most elegant car McLaren has produced, but its performances were mightily impressive. The driver in this shot is Ayrton Senna.

BELOW RIGHT
Senna in the wet, where he excelled – as in most other conditions. The car is an MP4/7A, the least successful of the Honda-engined McLarens (most other teams would have been overjoyed by the results achieved with it). Compared with MP4/5, the front suspension is cleaner and despite the need to house spring/damper units horizontally within the nose, this is also finer.

The first McLaren-Honda overwhelmed the 1988 championships, the second was only slightly less dominant, the winning margin was less in 1990 and 1991. Four different engines were used, evidence of the resources Honda deployed to ensure success.

McLaren's liaison with Honda took shape through 1987, when Honda reworked its turbo engine for only one season's racing, as turbochargers were to be banned from 1989. Steve Nichols was McLaren's project leader, and the MP4/4 had no chassis or suspension novelties. However, transmission was through McLaren's new six-speed gearbox.

Ayrton Senna won eight GPs in 1988, and Alain Prost seven, and the McLaren pair were inevitably first and second in the Drivers' Championship. McLaren scored 199 points in the Constructors' Championship, while the next six teams on the final points table scored 192 between them – that emphasized a superiority not achieved before, even by the mighty German teams of the 1930s.

Neil Oatley headed the MP4/5 design group,

and this 1989 car had smoother lines clothing a new monocoque, while it was powered by Honda's 3.5-litre V10, credited with an output approaching 700 bhp. There was a 'B' version for 1990, with a similar specification, although its monocoque incorporated new impact-resistant materials, and there were aerodynamic refinements as the search for fractional advantages continued.

In 1989 Senna won six GPs and Prost won four, but the French driver took the title. Senna was undisputed number one driver in the team in 1990 and with six GP wins he regained the title, while his new team mate Gerhard Berger was only fourth. The makes title was McLaren's in both years.

The third engine of the alliance came for 1991, a 60-degree 3.5-litre V12 that was to be substantially revised during the season. At the start of the year its output exceeded 700 bhp. The MP4/6 had revised monocoque and suspension, and aerodynamics that were improved as experience suggested minor shortcomings. Resources allowed for two R & D

programmes through the year – a semi-automatic transmission on the basis of the transverse six-speed gearbox normally used, and an active suspension system (not used until late 1992).

The reward was a record-setting fourth championship for the team, while with seven GP victories Senna comfortably topped the drivers' points list again, to the extent that he was able to hand the Japanese GP victory to team mate Berger.

The MP4/7A for 1992 had another new monocoque, the semi-automatic transmission and a 75-degree Honda V12, with pneumatic valve operation among its novelties (following a Renault lead, as a means to achieve higher revs). However, it was little more powerful than rival power units, and had a greater thirst for fuel, which translates into higher start-line weights. By the high 1988-91 standards McLaren set with the three previous Honda engines, 1992 was disappointing: the drivers won only five GPs (Senna three, Berger two) and the team was well beaten into second in the Constructors' Championship.

Honda turned away from Formula 1 at the end of that year, ending a most fruitful association. In five seasons, the McLaren-Hondas had scored 699 championship points.

Ferrari 640

RIGHT and BELOW
The Ferrari 640 was a distinctive car. These are driven by Mansell, at the Paul Ricard circuit and at Monaco.

In terms of Grand Prix victories, Ferrari slumped in the mid-1980s, with just three wins in 1984-86, and that led to a fresh approach. It paid dividends, in three 1989 victories and then in 1990 Ferrari had its best season since 1979, as six GPs fell to the red cars.

The most radical move in the late 1980s was the establishment of an advanced design centre (GTO) under John Barnard in England. The first GTO design was the 639, tested in 1988 but never raced, and leading to the 640 for 1989. In this, Ferrari returned to a V12 engine, a 65-degree 3-litre unit for which 600 bhp was claimed as the season opened and 660 bhp by its end. Barnard pushed through the adoption of an electro-hydraulic gearchange, with two finger-pressure levers ahead of the steering wheel for up and down changes and a clutch pedal used only when starting from rest. The carbon-composite monocoque was slender, and the sides of the car bulged for aerodynamic reasons.

Mansell drove a 640 to a debut race victory in Brazil in 1989, surprising at the time and the more surprising in view of the teething problems that followed. Then there were two mid-season wins and at the end of the year Ferrari was third in the Constructors' Championship.

Steve Nichols took on the design role late in 1989, and sensibly made as few changes as possible in the 641, primarily revising the chassis and body to accommodate a larger fuel cell and improve aerodynamic qualities. In 1990 Alain Prost won five GPs while Mansell won just one, and Ferrari was the convincing runner-up in the Constructors' Championship.

It all turned to ashes in 1991, when Ferrari started the season with the 642/2 and completed it with the 643 which inherited many features. The team failed to win a race, and was not competitive again until 1993.

Williams-Renault

BELOW
BELOW
The FW16 evolved from the FW15, with unseen torsion bar springs at the front and an eye-catching aerodynamic arrangement at the rear which included the lower wing with pronounced anhedral. This car is driven by David Coulthard, who showed confidence to back up ability when he raced the cars after Ayrton Senna's fatal accident at Imola.

RIGHT
An FW15D with a colour scheme emphasizing the broad side pods. The cockpit surround fits tightly around Damon Hill.

Grand Prix cars reached a technological peak in 1993, then designers were reined in by the governing body. That year, the Williams-Renault FW15C was perhaps the most sophisticated car ever raced, yet under Technical Director Patrick Head, the team was looking forward to more fundamental innovations, plans which then gathered dust.

The team's downbeat season in 1987 turned out to be an interlude while collaboration with Renault was finalized. The French RS1 V10 ran its first circuit tests in the Autumn of 1988, and was used in the FW12C and FW13 in 1989. That year Thierry Boutsen won the Canadian and Australian GPs for Williams, and the team was runner-up in the Makes Championship; 1990 was not a good year as there were weaknesses in the FW13, and although Patrese and Boutsen each won a race the team's final championship position was fourth.

In 1991 the FW14 had Renault's RS3 V10, delivering up to 770 bhp at revs that would have been scarcely credible a decade earlier – 14,500 rpm was quoted. Nigel Mansell returned to Williams to win five GPs, while Patrese won two; in the makes contest, Williams was runner-up to McLaren.

The next three seasons were Williams'. In 1992 there was the FW14B, with the V10 output rated no higher, which gave Mansell the Driver's Championship (with nine victories), while the ever-reliable Patrese won once, and Williams took the constructors' title by a massive margin. That was even greater – double the runner-up score – in 1993, when Prost won the driver's title in his final GP season with seven GP wins, and Damon Hill came into the team, to win three times.

The first two marginally-different versions of FW15 were not raced, for under Patrick Head's

direction, the ultra-efficient team had FW15C available for the 1993 season. Its Renault RS5 was an over-square unit, with the large valves combined with the pneumatic valve closing developed on RS4, and with components such as lightweight pistons, the capability to rev to 15,000 rpm, and the specialized fuel brews permitted into 1993, made it an 800 bhp engine. It drove through a Williams six-speed gearbox, and the change was sequential (up or down, a gear could not be 'skipped') and could be automatic or semi-automatic, with a driver-operated finger-tip control on the steering wheel. Throttle control was an electronic 'fly-by-wire' system, with no mechanical linkages. The engine management system synchronized engine speed and gear changes and also cut out wasteful wheel spin at a start.

The carbon fibre/Kevlar monocoque closely followed FW14, as did the refined hydro-pneumatic 'active' suspension, in which computer-controlled hydraulic jacks took the place of springs and dampers. A driver could adjust this during a race.

In 1993 Prost put a Williams on pole for 13 races, while Hill took two pole positions in his first full GP season. Between them they won ten GPs, Prost gaining his fourth world title.

The team had the FW16 in 1994, a simplified evolutionary car as most computerized systems had been banned. There were aerodynamic and rear suspension problems, but these were overshadowed when the team had to fight back after Senna's fatal accident. Hill won four GPs, but was beaten to the Drivers' Championship by one point. David Coulthard made his mark, contributing 14 points to Williams' championship score while Mansell scored 13 (ten as he won the final GP of the year).

In six seasons, the Williams-Renault combination won 37 Grands Prix and its drivers scored 709 points, and there were three Constructors' Championships. It continued as a leading force under new 3-litre regulations into 1995.

Lola T93

RIGHT
Nigel Mansell cornering the Newman-Haas Lola T93 very energetically, during his scintillating rookie season in 1993.

BELOW
Pit stop frenzy as Mario Andretti makes a routine stop at Nazareth in 1993.

BELOW RIGHT
The angle of this shot accentuates the needle nose of the T93. The regulation manifold pressure relief valve ('pop-off valve') projects above the rear bodywork. Indy car rules mean that rear aerofoil heights varied, for road circuits or fast tracks.

The Indianapolis 500 first fell to a Lola in 1966, when Graham Hill won in a T90 'American Red Ball Special'. But the marque's next win in the American Classic did not come until 1978, when Al Unser won in a Cosworth DFX-engined T500 – Cosworth's first victory in the race. During a period of change in American racing, the CART championship gained in stature, yet its origins were recognized in the Indycar term, which became the official title in 1992. Rule changes that year led to a new Lola, the T92, which carried the then-new Cosworth XB to its first race wins.

Generalizing, Indy cars looked like F1 machines, a little larger and with more variation in aerofoils, small on fast ovals, large on road circuits. Some sophisticated components were banned, to keep costs under control, but 'ground effects' were allowed. The 2.67-litre (161.7 cu in) turbocharged eight-cylinder engines burnt methanol fuel and gave some 800-850 bhp, and as tank capacity was limited to 40 gallons

refuelling remained as much a feature of this type of racing as it had always been.

The Lola T92 for 1992 was conventional, built around a monocoque chassis. The Rahal-Hogan team that fielded the T92 for Indycar champion Bobby Rahal used Ilmor-Chevrolet units, while the Newman-Haas and Ganassi teams used the Cosworth XB; Michael Andretti started winning in Newman-Haas T92s in mid-season.

The T93 was a development of the proven T92, and the Newman-Haas cars dominated the 1993 season. Nigel Mansell drove them to take the World Series Championship in a sensational rookie season, with six race wins, while his team mate Mario Andretti won his last Indycar race with one. Other winning T93 drivers were Danny Sullivan and Al Unser Jr. in Galles team cars with Chevrolet V8s. The 1994 Indianapolis start line up included 19 T93s and 8 T92s, and they took 9 of the first 10 places. The next year saw Lola eclipsed.

Benetton-Ford

A B194 during early-1994 tests. One of the outrigged aerodynamic fences can be seen behind the front wheel. Intended to direct the airflow, these became widely used in the mid-1990s. The fuel intake behind the cockpit locates the point where the horrifying fire in the pits during the German GP started, as the hose was uncoupled from it and because a filter was missing some fuel sprayed onto and around the car.

Benetton entered the world of Grand Prix racing as a sponsor with Tyrrell in 1983, and from 1986 the name of this Italian clothing company was also the name of a British Formula 1 constructor, as it took over the Toleman team and its base, together with talented designer Rory Byrne.

After a year with BMW turbo engines in the B186, and a victory in the Mexican GP, Benetton turned to an association with Ford that lasted until 1994. For 1987 the Ford-Cosworth turbo V6 was used in the B187, with a third placing the best result before adoption of the normally-aspirated 3.5-litre Ford Cosworth DFR led to a third new car, B188.

This was conventional, and was used in active suspension trials – a sign that Benetton was a serious constructor. It was overweight and the engine was by no means the most powerful on the 1988-89 grids, but in 1988 Boutsen was third in six GPs, Nannini in two, and the points accrued meant that Benetton was third in the Constructors' Championship, although its points score was modest.

Ford's HB 75-degree V8 was compact and light, and the equal of most 1989 engines. In mid-season Benetton introduced the B189, carefully packaged around it. Alessandro Nannini scored his only GP victory in a B189, in Japan.

The B189 was used on into 1990, while the B190 was developed. This was under the control of ex-McLaren, ex-Ferrari designer John Barnard, and his influence showed most in aerodynamic respects, although the monocoque and suspension were also new. The HB was uprated, to give some 650 bhp in mid-season, and that was enough to make the B190 really competitive

(Nelson Piquet drove it to GP victories in Japan and Australia).

Barnard left in 1991, Byrne returned; Tom Walkinshaw's TWR gained a stake in Benetton, and brought designer Ross Brawn. The B191 had a new chassis and bodywork which featured a high nose (following a Tyrrell example), with the V8 giving 730 bhp, but with inadequate tyres. Piquet won the Canadian GP, and to a furore about contracts, Michael Schumacher joined the team.

The B192 had little 'new' about it – notably, no active suspension or automatic transmission – but it was quick and reliable. Benetton scored points at every GP, Schumacher gained his first GP victory in Belgium, Martin Brundle contributed to the team's third place in the Makes Championship by scoring in the last nine races.

There were advanced technical components such as active suspension, a six-speed semi-automatic gearbox and traction control on the B193. The potential in car and driver were shown with fastest laps in five GPs, but some reliability was lost, so there was just one GP

victory for Schumacher in 1993 and third place in the Constructors' Cup again.

In 1994, team supremo Flavio Briatore, succeeded in obtaining Renault engines for 1995, ironically as Benetton was at last the pace-setting team. Ford's high-revving Zetec-R matched the rest, so did the B194, which was simpler than B193, as some of the electronic high technology had been banned.

On the down side, Benetton was often under a cloud of controversy. There were questions about the programmes in electronic black boxes, there was a spectacular pits fire after refuelling equipment was 'modified', there was Schumacher's exclusion from three races, and his disqualification in Belgium. Despite all that, eight GPs fell to the German driver, and he secured the drivers' title at the last race, again in circumstances some regarded as questionable. Justice seemed to be done as Benetton was only second in the Constructors' Cup, in a season when it more than doubled its score of championship victories – seven between 1986 and 1993, eight in 1994.

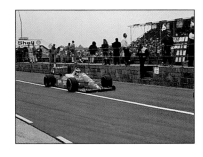

ABOVE
A Benetton B188 at the end of its racing life, being driven out of the Silverstone pits by Emanuele Pirro in 1989. The broad-chord front wing had the 'curly' trailing edge favoured by designer Byrne.

BELOW
The B193 was unquestionably distinctive, although by 1993 other constructors had taken up the underslung front wing layout. The driver is Michael Schumacher.

Penske PC23

Roger Penske was one of the leading personalities of CART – Championship Auto Racing Teams – when it was set up in 1978, in a split with the 'traditional' USAC Indianapolis reactionaries. Broadly the rift was to be healed, but one legacy was variations in regulations, and Penske was to exploit this in 1994.

Quite simply, the team had the resources to use the Ilmor-D dohc 2.65-litre 740 bhp V8 through 15 of the championship races, and take advantage of the more generous Indianapolis capacity allowance for single-cam pushrod engines: Penske adopted the 3.4-litre Mercedes-Benz-labelled but Ilmor-built and developed 500I V8, which would be the most powerful in that most important 500-mile race - its first race.

Chief designer Nigel Bennett, based at Penske's Poole manufacturing plant, and his engineers on both sides of the Atlantic,

developed the 1993 chassis and suspension for the PC23. The new Ilmor engines were smaller, which made for tighter rear bodywork and better aerodynamics (Indy car aerofoil restrictions were stricter in 1994). Although the car was conventional, it was the product of a dedicated team, and a designer whose cars (Lola and Penske) had already won 61 CART races.

To back that, Penske ran three cars in 1994. Al Unser Jr. scored seven wins in the Ilmor D-engined cars, Canadian Paul Tracy contributed three wins and Fittipaldi won just once. Unser, Fittipaldi and Tracy were 1-2-3 in the end-of-season points listing.

Meanwhile, the 'Mercedes'-powered cars had set the pace at Indianapolis, Unser and Fittipaldi both leading. The Brazilian crashed in the final phase, leaving Unser to score the Penske team's tenth victory at the Speedway.

ABOVE
'Powered by Mercedes-Benz' on the engine cover shows that this PC23 is at Indianapolis, with one of the Penske-commissioned, Ilmor-built, Mercedes-named V8s. It also has the smaller aerofoils mandatory on high-speed tracks. The driver is Emerson Fittipaldi, who was challenging team mate Al Unser Jr. for the lead in the '500' when he crashed.

RIGHT
Champion Al Unser Jr. with a PC23 in 'road-circuit' trim (with large aerofoils) at Portland in June 1994.